**What Others Are Saying
about *Old Testament Prophets:
Their Connection to
New Testament Prophecy and
Their Relevance Today***

Have you ever wanted to know more about who the prophets of the Old Testament are? Wonder no longer. Jim Manthey introduces you to them, including information on where they lived and the consequences of their calling. Not some dry textbook, Jim's descriptions will keep you reading, hungering to know if these men who lived long ago were all that much different from you and me today. You will find out that, in many ways, they were quite similar. We should not be surprised since the epistle of James addresses this issue (James 5:10–11, 17–18). You will want to add this book to your other study materials on the Bible, and you will use it as a reference tool in days and years to come. The author has also set up the information in such a way that you can readily utilize it in your study groups. Questions at the end of each chapter lend themselves well for this purpose.

—Valerie Jean Routhieaux, author of *Scarred*,
Manifest Destiny, and *Stowaway*.

After reviewing and enjoying Jim Manthey's study on the prophets, I would like to say that this is a fresh look at the connection between the prophecies of the Old and New Testaments. Any person studying the end times will find the information gathered here helpful in their understanding of New Testament prophecy. This material will be particularly useful for Bible study leaders, Sunday school teachers, and for personal use. I especially like Jim's addition of a rhyming poem for each prophet.

—Jim Underhill—Bible college graduate,
Sunday school teacher, neighborhood Bible study leader,
and a member of Gideons International.

Jim Manthey has obviously invested a great deal of time and effort in this book: its content, its organization, and even its design. He has prepared the book in a logical way that facilitates its use. He has fulfilled the promise in the title by giving us a broad view of the Old Testament prophets, relating each to material in the book of Revelation, and then showing the relevance of the content to current faith and worship. This book will be a valuable guide to those of us with limited skills in reading the OT and limited comprehension of its significance in our Christian lives. I recommend it for private study, for use in groups such as adult Bible classes and as a reference that one can go back to repeatedly to retrieve information. With this recommendation, I suggest that users pay close attention to the notes at the end of each section. Of course, these are meant to enable deeper study as they do, but Manthey has embedded in these notes important information that appears nowhere else, including resources not listed in the bibliography. So use it all!

—Frances Fuller, retired missionary, author of *In Borrowed Houses* (a true story of love and faith amidst war in Lebanon), winner of: the Illumination Bronze Medal for memoir, the Grand Prize winner in the 50 Great Writers You Should Be Reading contest, and first place memoir in the Northern California Publishers and Authors competition.

OLD TESTAMENT
PROPHETS

JAMES MANTHEY

OLD TESTAMENT
PROPHETS

*Their Connection to New Testament
Prophecy, Their Relevance Today*

TATE PUBLISHING
AND ENTERPRISES, LLC

Published by Tate Publishing & Enterprises, LLC
127 E. Trade Center Terrace | Mustang, Oklahoma 73064 USA
1.888.361.9473 | www.tatepublishing.com

Tate Publishing is committed to excellence in the publishing industry. The company reflects the philosophy established by the founders, based on Psalm 68:11,

"The Lord gave the word and great was the company of those who published it."

Book design copyright © 2015 by Tate Publishing, LLC. All rights reserved.
Cover design by Jim Villaflores
Interior design by Manolito Bastasa

Published in the United States of America

ISBN: 978-1-68164-668-8
Religion / Biblical Studies / Prophets
15.09.07

I dedicate this work to four dear friends: Jim and Ann Jacobson, together with their son Christian, as well as Jim's mother, "Mom J." Thanks, Jacobsons, for your faithfulness in doing our weekly study of the Old Testament prophets. Ann's later courage in battling health challenges has also been an inspiration to all. She has held faithful to God, trusting in his mercy throughout. Now, by God's grace, the Lord has healed her!

Acknowledgments

I want to thank Valerie Routhieaux, an author in her own right, for her comprehensive overhaul of the entire manuscript. Your corrections and encouragement went way beyond what I expected. Thanks, Valerie. The passage from the Sermon on the Mount comes to mind: "Whoever compels you to go one mile, go with him two" (Matt. 5:41, NKJV).

Contents

Foreword

WHAT WILL YOU gain by a study of the Old Testament prophets? I think that often, the prophets go unread. Either they are too long and involved (like the major prophets Isaiah, Jeremiah, and Ezekiel) or they are too short and obscure (like the minor prophets Obadiah and Habakkuk), Christians might reason. They are also part of the Old Testament in a day and age when most want to focus on the New. As a result, a legitimate fear is that they do not get enough ink, except to point out when someone like the Apostle Paul or our Lord Jesus Christ himself. Therefore, let this be an exercise in bringing the prophets to the forefront. This study aims to effect a rich, vibrant appreciation for the Bible and for Old Testament prophecy in particular, including its relevance for us yet today.

Of interest to those who wish to look into this further: The Bible itself speaks of prophets and prophesying in dif-

ferent contexts. In Acts 2:17–18, Peter, filled with the Holy
Spirit on Pentecost Day, first day of the New Testament
church, quotes a Joel passage (Joel 2:28–32) in describing
how, in the last days, sons, daughters, young men, and old
men shall prophesy, see visions, and have dreams. 1 John
4:1 warns against false prophets and encourages us to "test
the spirits." In 1 Corinthians 12:28–29, it reminds us of the
elevated stature of the prophets which is "cemented" (if you
get the pun) in an Ephesians 2:20 passage listing the prophets as among those forming the church's foundation. In
Acts 2:25–31, a further portion of Peter's great Pentecostal
sermon, David is cited as being prophetic through his fre-
quent predictions of the Messiah, Jesus Christ. In 2 Peter
2:12–22, finally, describes in great detail what prophecy
doesn't look or sound like, ending in the well-remembered
image of a "dog returning to its own vomit" (NASB, verse
22) to describe those who delight in following "the way of
Balaam" (NASB, verse 15).

A spur for greater attention given to the prophets is
that there are several similarities between passages from
both John's New Testament book on the end of times
(Revelation) and from the prophets of old. This should not
surprise since John, like all authors of the New Testament,
had been brought up on the Old Testament law, prophets and writings, called by Jewish people the TaNaKh
(an acronym for Torah or law, Nevi'im or prophets, and

Ketuvim or writings). The earlier more common name, actually, was miqra. Others have noticed the similarities as well. I was delighted recently to see, for instance, that Kay Arthur in her popular book, *How To Study Your Bible*, has commented in detail on the phenomenon of Old Testament prophecies popping up all over in the New Testament of any study Bible, showing the many overlaps between the two. This must be part of the source, then, of the well-known saying, "The Old Testament is the New Testament concealed; while the New Testament is the Old Testament revealed."

Theologians often speak of the threefold ministry of Jesus Christ: prophet, priest, and king. In a book on the prophets, we cannot but highlight how Jesus was the greatest of all prophets as well as the one all prophets pointed to—both the Old Testament prophets and John, in Revelation (in the latter case, "pointing" to Jesus' second coming).

One of the most exciting examples of our Lord and Savior acting in his role as prophet has to be the event recorded in Luke 4:18. Here, fresh from his defeat of the devil's threefold temptation in the wilderness, Jesus was at the beginning of a three-year ministry that would culminate in His sacrificial death for our sins and resurrection. In so doing, he would change the world forever, fulfilling over three hundred prophecies of his coming and bringing eternal life to all who would believe.

On this occasion, he was in Galilee, among His family and hometown crowd. He went into the synagogue on a Sabbath day (setting a precedent for both his own ministry and, later, the Apostle Paul's). He began reading from Isaiah 61:1: "The Spirit of the Lord is upon me." The New Testament was revealing the Old in the strongest way possible: the prediction of the prophet regarding the Messiah was coming true before people's very eyes. What proved difficult for many of them was that, despite news of his miracles and amazingly authoritative teaching, He was one of them, brought up in their home territory. Only later, especially after he had risen from the dead, did many believe, including his own siblings. Brother James, then, became a pillar of the early church in Jerusalem, finally sacrificing his own life rather than renounce his faith.

The question may be asked: Is there a way to present the great prophecies of the Bible in a way that causes us to better grasp the essentials and capture some of the beauty and majesty God's spokesperson must have felt when writing? The Lord has moved me, I believe, to generate a format presenting the truths of Scripture in such a way. With the Spirit's help, our heightened curiosity will more likely bear fruit leading to further study and discussion. My prayer is that the Spirit will work through the suggestions here to lead the reader also to a place of self-discovery, going hand in hand with a closer relationship to Jesus.

A guiding principle, as in all biblical scholarship, has been to follow rules of good exegesis, guarding against the temptation to read things into passages that the divinely inspired author did not want but only pulling out what the biblical writer intended.[1]

Some aspects of the strategy used here include opening each book with a Hebrew passage, deemed representative of the prophet in question. The Hebrew passages are for those wishing to keep alive their knowledge of the original language or for those curious enough just to see what the original looks like. I deemed the chosen Hebrew passage representative of the message God gave his representative to share with his people.

Then I made a decision to list some of the background and other literary features specific to each prophetical book. By recognizing and pointing out literary, historical, and other points of interest, we can gain more insight into the message, the times, and the spiritual significance of each representative for the Lord: "They, Wisdom's words, are life to those who find them" (Prov. 4:22). I highlighted the end of this opening section, however, by a connection to words and actions of our Savior as recorded in the Gospel accounts. In so doing, we emphasize how each prophet, just as each of us, must bow his knee in worship and dependence upon Jesus as the Messiah, Lord, and Savior of all— both Old and New Testament believers.

Some chapters have additional informative material specific to the prophet. Included among the latter, at times, is the citing of popular, well-known passages. By isolating and highlighting key or famous passages, listed in their order of occurrence, we can gain a better acquaintance with the message at large of each man of God. When you learn to like, even love someone, you want to know more about them. One benefit of becoming better acquainted with the prophets (and therefore with Jesus, who quoted the prophets constantly) is "That you may observe discretion and your lips may reserve knowledge" (Prov. 5:2).

Next, I highlighted parallel passages from the prophet under study and Revelation. To do this, I placed discovered and chosen parallel passages in a side-by-side format. Comparing the two, we come to see, I think, a specific example, from the word, that Jesus Christ is "the same yesterday, today and forever" (Heb. 13:8).

In a third column, I prayerfully derived, beside the two parallel passages, an application. Applications help bring home in a more personal way such biblical truths as "This is the work of God that you believe in him whom he has sent" (John 6:29).

The review question section at the end of each prophet will help you solidify the salient facts of each book and maybe learn and retain some things you didn't already know.

Finally, a summary of the prophetic message, theology, and, sometimes, history appears. For those with a history of an Isaiah or Jeremiah scaring them away due to their length, it is an attempt to summarize and capsulize, in a form that resonates, in poetic form, at the end of each prophet section. For those who like poetry, I hope you will enjoy. Despite the poetic format and obvious effort at crafting words to fit the rhyming pattern, keeping true to the rules of good exegesis was still the primary driving force. Pull out what the Bible says, and don't read in anything that isn't really there. I abandoned rhyming schemes, in fact, where an attempt at rhyming would have threatened good exegesis. Only occasionally did I delve into the mind of the prophet where I thought the first-person musings might bring the reader closer into the pathos of the moment. The first-person laments of Jeremiah in Lamentations were the one time this happened. The poem of Ezekiel also utilizes this technique partially. The Bible is truly Basic Information Before Leaving Earth (BIBLE). Like a map to the pathfinder, or a compass to the orienteer, God's precious word, true to the last iota, promises to point us in the direction of God's will for our lives: "Your word is a lamp to my feet and a light to my path" (Ps. 119:105). Finally, and once again, what do the Old Testament prophets have to say about Jesus Christ, our salvation through Christ, our relationship with God because of all that Christ has done for us? They all have much to say, and this should be our focus. Look everywhere for hints of the Messiah, or the *mashiach* (as Hebrew pronounces the word).

—Jim Manthey

Chronology of the Old Testament Prophets

Prophet	Dates of Ministry	Kingdom and Kings	Scripture
Samuel[1]	Ca. 1100–1012 BC	Israel: David and Saul	1 Samuel 25:1, 28:3
Obadiah	848–841 BC	Judah: Jehoram, Ahaziah, Athaliah	2 Kings: 8–12; 2 Chronicles: 21–24
Joel[2]	835–796 BC	Judah: Joash	2 Kings 12; 2 Chronicles 24
Jonah	793–753 BC	Israel: Jeroboam 2	2 Kings 14
Amos	760–753 BC	Israel: Jeroboam 2	2 Kings 14
Hosea	760–720 BC	Israel: Jeroboam 2, Zechariah, Shallum Judah: Menahem, Pekahiah, Pekah, Hoshea	2 Kings 14–17

Isaiah	740–681 BC	Judah: Uzziah, Jotham, Ahaz, Hezekiah, Manasseh	2 Kings 15–21; 2 Chronicles 26–33
Micah	735–700 BC	Judah: Jotham, Ahaz, Hezekiah	2 Kings 15–20; 2 Chronicles 27–32
Nahum	664–654 BC	Judah: Manasseh	2 Kings 21–23; 2 Chronicles 33–35
Zephaniah	632–628 BC	Judah: Josiah	2 Kings 22–23; 2 Chronicles 34–35
Jeremiah	627–580 BC	Judah: Josiah, Jehoahaz, Jehoiakim, Jehoiachin, Zedekiah Babylon: Nebuchadnezzar	2 Kings 22–25 2 Chronicles 34–36
Habakkuk	609–605 BC	Judah: Josiah, Jehoahaz, Jehoiakim,	2 Kings 22–24; 2 Chronicles 34–36
Daniel	605–534 BC	Judah: Jehoiakim; Babylon: Nebuchadnezzar, Belshazzar; Persia: Darius 1, Cyrus	2 Kings 23–25; 2 Chronicles 36; Ezra 1–4
Ezekiel	593–571 BC	Judah: Zedekiah Babylon: Nebuchadnezzar	2 Kings 24–25; 2 Chronicles 3
Haggai	520 BC	Zerubbabel; Persia: Darius 1	Ezra 5–6

Zechariah	520–480 BC	Zerubbabel; Persia: Darius 1, Xerxes	Ezra 5–6
Malachi	432–425 BC	Persia: Artaxerxes, Darius 2	Ezra 7, Nehemiah 6

As we look at the timeline, it is interesting to note the over-lap of prophets, meaning that these mouthpieces of the Lord were contemporaries: Jonah, Amos, and Hosea, for instance. Hosea, Isaiah, and Micah are another example, not to mention Jeremiah, Habakkuk, and Daniel. Daniel and Ezekiel may have known one another while in exile in Babylonia. A teenaged Daniel had been included in the first wave of captives while Babylon shipped off Ezekiel in the second wave. Meanwhile, Jeremiah, although given the option to come to Babylon and enjoy a favored status (he had urged his people and the king to surrender and was rewarded, therefore, by Nebuchadnezzar with choices—the mercy of God also working in his favor) was forced instead, by the politics of those fleeing to Egypt, to accompany the latter.

When the Lord had moved world events to allow for the prophesied return from Babylon, Haggai and Zechariah were involved in God's command to rebuild the temple in Jerusalem. Others were the only ones called for their time: Samuel, Obadiah, and Joel (assuming the conservative view of Joel's earlier appearance is true). Add to the latter group Nahum, Zephaniah, and Malachi, finally.

Another division of the twelve minor prophets includes those from the Assyrian period: Hosea, Joel, Amos, Obadiah, Jonah, and Micah; three from the time of Assyria's decline: Nahum, Habakkuk, and Zephaniah; finally, those serving during the postexilic time (three once again): Haggai, Zechariah, and Malachi.[4,5]

The writing prophets, finally, found here were the ones who ended up leaving us with a book authored by them, through the Holy Spirit's anointing and power. Elijah and Elisha are included, though they never authored their own book. Other prophets mentioned throughout Scripture did not achieve that distinction.

Nathan, at the time of David, comes to mind in that respect; Shemaiah (2 Chron. 11:2), sent to evil Rehoboam is another. Uriah, son of Shemaiah, mentioned on Jeremiah 26:20–23, was slain by wicked King Jehoiakim, after having been tracked down by henchmen of the same. Let's not forget the one hundred anonymous prophets hidden from a vengeful Jezebel by the good and godly man, Obadiah, as described in 1 Kings 18:1–4. In addition, schools of prophets are described in 2 Kings 2, as the time for Elijah's rapture was approaching. Others had gifts of prophecy, but we do not consider them prophets. Joseph, with his gift of dreams, is an example. Not even worthy of consideration were the false prophets, many of whom fell under divine censure and terminal punishment.

Notes

1. Many attribute his statement to St. Augustine.
2. The rules of good exegesis would include considering the context. Don't derive meaning from information that is out of context. Interpret literally most things unless there is good reason to read the passage as figurative language. This is especially important in the symbolic language of eschatology and the more obscure prophetic passages—as in Daniel's visions. Be familiar with the culture, history, and customs of the time described.
3. Many reckon Samuel's date of birth at 1105. Hannah weaned him for a time. He then began his ministry at the temple, first under Eli then by himself for the rest of his life. Many reckon Saul's death around 1010 BC. Assuming Samuel died ten years before Saul that would put Samuel's death at 1020 BC. In addition, the original compiler of this timeline did not include Samuel, presumably because Samuel is not listed in any of the texts of Scripture as among the prophetic books.
4. Modern critics date Obadiah late—post-exilic.
5. Merrill F. Unger, *Unger's Bible Handbook* (Chicago: Moody Press, 1967), 403. Also: Some want to put Obadiah between the Babylonian attacks on the City of David (605–586 BC) NASB Study Bible (Zondervan Publishing House, 1995), 124.

Samuel blesses the first king of Israel, Saul.

Samuel

כי שמואל את־שמו ותקרא בן ותלד   מייהוה שאלתי

And she [Hannah, Elkanah's wife] gave birth
to a son and she named him Samuel [the name
means] "[Because I have] asked him of the Lord."

—1 Samuel 1:20 (NASB)

SAMUEL IS UNIQUE among the Old Testament prophets.
He wore many hats, more than anyone else did. He was a
prophet, priest, and judge. Perhaps most remember him as
a priest, the young boy who grew up in the synagogue com-
plex, a child dedicated by his mother, the latter grateful that
God would grant her a son after some years of barrenness.
He lived in the waning years of the eleventh century BC, as
the years, from our vantage point, prepared to change from
a four-digit to a three-digit number. The fact that Samuel

was born at all was a miracle in itself. He was the answer
to a prayer from his previously barren mother, Hannah, one
of two wives of Elkanah. In her barrenness, she joins an
honored list including the likes of Abraham's Sarah, Isaac's
Rebecca, and Jacob's Rachel. The other wife in the account
of Samuel, who had no problem bearing children, was
Peninnah. In this story, Peninnah was having all the children in the beginning (like Abraham's Hagar and Jacob's
Leah). You can find the story in 1 Samuel 1:1–6, 1:20, and
2:1–3 (the latter sometimes referred to as "The Magnificat"
of the Old Testament). Compare Hanna's song of joy with
Mary's New Testament song in Luke 1:76–77.[1]

Other prophets who had more than one office include
Jeremiah, from Anatoth then Jerusalem, who ministered
from 626 BC to 586 BC, who was a priest first then a prophet.
Ezekiel, who prophesied during the Babylonian captivity some four hundred years after Samuel, was a prophet
and priest as well, although his priestly functions were
curtailed by the captivity crisis. Daniel, from roughly the
same period as Ezekiel, was a prophet and public official.
Zechariah returned to Judah in 538 BC from Babylon. Like
Jeremiah and Ezekiel before him, he was both prophet and
priest. Some think that Joel, about whom we know little,
may have doubled as a priest, besides his prophetic duties.

As for the historical background of 1 and 2 Samuel,
Samuel began serving in the temple under Eli, the Levitical

priest. He probably continued serving into his eighties or nineties. Samuel appears to be the author of 1 Samuel. The account of his death appears in chapter 25 of 1 Samuel. Therefore, the content of 2 Samuel (actually all part of one book originally) was continued by a different author, assuming Samuel's authorship of the first part.

Like Daniel and Jeremiah later, Samuel began his service as a young boy (the other two beginning more as teens). Eli was high priest at the time Samuel's parents brought him to the temple. The wickedness of Eli's sons (Hophni and Phinehas) was well documented (1 Sam. 2:22–25), contrast the righteousness of the boy, Samuel (1 Sam. 2:26).

Some stories coming to mind from Bible history that are concerned with blessings for the righteous and curses for the wicked include Cain and Abel, Jacob and Esau, Peter and Judas, and Jesus's parable of the talents (Matt. 25:14 ff).

The greatest reward for Samuel in heaven, we think, stems from his unflinching devotion to God and to the duties assigned to him. Perhaps his greatest honor comes from the Lord choosing him to anoint David as king— he from whom would descend our Lord and Savior, Jesus Christ.

The young boy, Samuel, in the temple brings to mind the boy Jesus in the temple showing a wisdom and knowledge beyond his years. It would not be surprising to think that our Heavenly Father uses images of godly, earthly men to set the stage for a later established and anointed appearance of the Messiah, Jesus Christ. Samuel learned to say "speak, Lord, your servant hears." Jesus prayed: "Your will be done." Samuel, who once served Levi the high priest, is now in heaven serving his Lord and Savior—the ultimate sacrificial lamb, Jesus Christ.

Samuel, a Nazirite?

Of all biblical men of note, Samson, Samuel and John the Baptist appear to have been Nazirites for life whose parents had taken a vow for them before they were able to make the choice themselves. The vow included abstaining from grapes and wine, shaving and haircutting as well as a prohibition on touching dead bodies. Restoration for broken vows was elaborate.[2]

The Call of Samuel

Contrast the call of Samuel in 1 Samuel chapter 3 with Elijah's talk with God after some time of being in His service (1 Kings 19:11 ff), or the call of Jeremiah described in Jeremiah 1:1–5.

Recap of the History of God's People under Samuel

1. Eventually, the Philistines capture the ark. Who are the Philistines? They are descended from a mysterious people historians like to call the sea peoples. Their arrival in Canaan dated back to 1200 BC. Their lands stretched from Joppa to south of Gaza. They were skilled in iron works and ships. They named Palestine after them. During the same battle in which Philistines captured the ark, the enemy also killed Hophni and Phinehas, Eli's wicked sons. Eli dies when he hears the news of the captured ark. Eli's daughter-in-law then dies in childbirth, completing the cycle of a curse pronounced earlier through Samuel upon the house of Eli. Other examples of people who died under curse by God due to wickedness include Ahab and Jezebel during the time of Elijah, also David and Bathsheba's child during the days of Nathan the prophet.

2. The curse of the ark while in the hands of the Philistines, I main cities of the Philistines were Gath, Ashkelon, Ekron, Gaza, and Ashdod.

3. A summary of Samuel's manifold ministry is 1 Samuel 7:13–17.

4. The Lord grants this wish, despite the fact of His will being to head a theocracy.

5. Samuel anoints Saul king (1 Sam. 10:1).

6. An example of Samuel's gift of prophecy is in 1 Samuel 10:3–7. This account reminds of the instructions given to Ananias concerning the Apostle Paul, after the latter's blinding on the road to Damascus (Acts 9:11). Better yet, recall Jesus's instructions to His disciples for obtaining the mule and upper room for the last supper (Luke 19:28 ff and 22:8–13).

7. Nearby enemies of God's people at this time included the Philistines, Amorites, Ammonites, and the Amalekites.

8. Samuel as a circuit judge—Ramah (home base), Bethel, Gilgal, and Mizpah (1 Sam. 7:15–17).

9. Sons of Samuel, Joel and Abijah, become judges also, but they end up corrupt like Hophni and Phinehas, sons of Eli. Other examples where the sons did not turn out as good as their fathers are Cain, son of Adam; Esau, son of Isaac; Absalom, son of King David; King Manasseh, son of King Hezekiah.

10. The rejection of Saul by God is in 1 Samuel 15:10–35 (yet the Lord allows him to reign a total of forty years—an example of why a day is as a thousand years and a thousand years as a day, to the Lord).

11. Samuel anoints David king (1 Sam. 16:1–13; 1029 BC).

12. David defeats Goliath and gains a following in Israel, leading to jealousy and friction with Saul (1 Sam. 17:23 ff)

13. A jealous Saul pursues David, trying to kill him (1 Sam. 19:1 ff).
14. The prophet, judge, and priest, Samuel, dies and is mourned by Israel (1 Sam. 25:1).
15. Samuel's spirit curses Saul through a medium (1 Sam. 28:15–20).
16. Saul and David's beloved friend, Jonathan, son of Saul, die in battle against the Philistines (1 Sam. 31: 1).

Samuel probably wrote much of 1 Samuel during Saul's reign. Abiathar, the priest, possibly completed the rest (including 2 Samuel). We recognize Samuel as one of the greatest leaders of all times in Israel (Jer. 15:1 and Heb. 11:38).

Comparison: Samuel, Revelation, and Application

Samuel	Revelation	Application
1 Samuel 3:1b The Word of the Lord was precious in those days. There was no open vision.	Revelation 1:10 I was in the Spirit on the Lord's day and heard behind me a great voice.	Today, God reveals himself to us in his word. 1 Corinthians 13:12
	Revelation 4:2 Immediately I was in the spirit: and behold, a throne was set in Heaven.	Now we see as through a glass dimly.
1 Samuel 2:12 Now the Sons of Eli were sons of Belial; they knew not the Lord.	Revelation 2:20 You tolerate that woman Jezebel. She leads my servants into sexual immorality.	1 Corinthians 5:6, Galatians 5:9 A little yeast leaven the whole lump; remove the immorality from your life, from your midst.

Samuel	Revelation	Application
1 Samuel 2:10c	Revelation 20:12c	On the day of judgment, all
The Lord will judge the ends of the earth.	The dead were judged from the things which were written in the books [the book of life and other books].	believers will be pronounced innocent through the blood of the Lamb.

Review Questions

Test your memory and understanding. Choose one.

1. What are the names of Eli's two sons? (Choose two: Hophni/ Phinehas, Joel/ Abijah) _____ and _____.
2. What was the name of Saul's father? (Samuel/Kish) _____.
3. What does the name *Samuel* mean? (Asked of the Lord/Blessed by God) _____.
4. The second chapter of 1 Samuel refers to Samuel's sons as "sons of (Belial/the devil) _____.'"
5. Name three offices or duties that Samuel held. (Choose three: shepherd/fisherman/prophet/priest/judge) _____ _____, _____, and _____.

How Samuel Is Still Relevant Today

The story of Samuel being forced to give the people what they wanted, despite his better judgment in knowing the granting of this request was going be accompanied by a lot of heartache, is not a new story. History repeats itself, and the events described in the Bible are no exception. How often have young people chosen for themselves a path their parents tried to warn them about and the outcome was, as predicted, full of sadness? A major thrust of Jesus's parable of the prodigal son centers around this theme. What has happened in the past and the lessons we can glean from them will apply in the lives of God's people until the end of times.[3]

The faithfulness and example of this great man of God will always serve as an inspiration, his life worthy of emulation, in Christ, for any child of God. Pastors and elders will not easily forget the blessings that are available, the rewards that just naturally flow, from a strong personal relationship with our God. From the close communion he enjoyed as a young boy where God spoke to Samuel in a dream to his later years when he was so in sync with God's will, he just always knew what the Lord wanted of him for his people before God even told him. Samuel remains a breath of fresh spiritual air to us all. We give thanks to our Lord for his life, his story, and his love for and devotion to God.

Samuel

Elkanah, son of Jeroham,
Hailed from Ephraim.
With *dalawang asawa*:[5]
Hannah and Peninnah.

The latter bore children,
The former none.
Elkanah loved Hannah more.
Though teasing from Peninnah wore thin.

Poor righteous Hanna!
Shades of Hagar and Sarah.
The righteous one endured,
Her sadness, through faithful prayer, cured.

Chided in prayer by even Eli
Who saw lips moving: wine?
"It's not wine or strong libations,"
She pleaded, "but, instead, my heart's palpitations."[6]

In the course of her petitions
To the God who is in accord.
She promised her son's dedication
To a life's service with the Lord.[7]

In short, God heard.
She bore a son.
Hannah's song of praise and thanks
The OT's "Magnificat" to some.[8]

"I asked him of the Lord"
(Mother Hannah rejoiced),
Giving reason for
Her son's name, in a word.

In temple quarters then,
Young Samuel trying to sleep;
"Samuel," Yahweh calls
Three times until Eli tells

The lad just what to say:
"Speak, Lord, your servant hears."
No doubt the message's implications
Left the boy on the verge of tears.

God opened young eyes quickly
When Yahweh at night came calling:
First mission, ministry—
To warn of Eli's falling.

Soon boy became a man:
A prophet, priest, and judge.
Bethel, Gilgal, Mizpah—
His circuit without grudge.

Then Israel too came calling
From blindness, for a king.
Their judge gave them a warning—
On deaf ears it fell, so sing.

Sing of monarchy and Saul.
Saul's end much like Goliath's—
The bigger's harder fall
Like Joel and Abijah, [9]

Faithful to the end,
To God his Lord and King
His judgment did not bend
To heaven him God did bring.

Notes

1. Ibid. mentions, page 357, that the normal period of service for a Leviticus priest would have been from twenty-five to fifty. Merrill Unger, *The New Unger's Bible Dictionary* (Chicago: Moody Press, 1988), 907, explains that the Nazirite vow could be for life or only for a short time. Hannah vowed the boy for a lifetime of service. The human psychology of a desperate, yet faithful, woman who wanted all the bargaining chips in her corner when in prayer to the Lord would allow for the maximum service. Her strong faith and love for God would argue, perhaps even more strongly, for a lifetime vow.

2. Ibid., 1121

3. *Nelson's Compact Bible Dictionary*, ed. Ronald F. Youngblood et al. (Nashville, Tennessee: Thomas Nelson, 2004), 542–544

4. Peter, in his second sermon as recorded in Acts 3, especially at Acts 3:18–23 and 3:24 ff, associates Samuel closely with the schools of prophets discussed here and in the study on Elijah of this same book.

5. Tagalog/Filipino for "two wives"

6. 1 Samuel 1:15–16.

7. The dedication was a Nazirite one.

8. NASB footnote, page 358

9. Joel and Abijah were sons of Samuel who did not walk in their father's footsteps. Their corruption became Israel's excuse for demanding a king—Merrill Unger, *The New Unger's Bible Dictionary* (Chicago: Moody Press, 1988), 6 and 696.

*Dore print of Elijah being raptured into heaven,
leaving behind his protégé and successor, Elisha.*

Elijah

אחאב אל־אליהו המצאתני איבי   ויאמר

Ahab said to Elijah,
"Have you found me, O my enemy?"

—1 Kings 21:20 (NASB)

THE NAME ELIJAH means "the Lord is my God." He lived in the ninth century BC. We find his story in 1 Kings and in the early part of 2 Kings. There is a statue of Elijah on Mount Carmel today, commemorating his victory over the prophets of Baal.[1]

Elijah is given favored status by the Lord such as was given to few others. The power to raise someone from the dead is an example. The authority to slaughter 750 false prophets was not commonplace either (although Samuel finished such a job for Saul the time that Saul neglected to follow God's entire command to slay Agag, king of the Amalekites. Samuel then had the enemy king cut into pieces.) The fact that God took Elijah into heaven and he did not see death (raptured) only occurred one other time in Scripture that we know of—Enoch. Finally, some think that one of the two witnesses spoken of in Revelation 11, just before the blowing of the seventh trumpet (part of the tribulation), may be Elijah brought back to earth. If true, the Lord uses him for special service, once again wreaking vengeance on several of the Lord's enemies at the end of times (Rev. 11:5). Again, Elijah's special reward from the Lord in heaven will surely derive from his faithful carrying out of all God's commands (although some he could not complete before his rapture, which Elisha, then, had to follow through with). He obeyed, that is, in spite of the personal danger he incurred from wicked King Ahab and Queen Jezebel.

The following is a list, in roughly chronological order, of the main events that took place during the ministry of Elijah. I will assign each event a message, association, or moral assessment:

Event	Message/Association
King Ahab marries Jezebel, a wicked Sidonian princess, contrary to God's command not to intermarry with pagans.	Do not get entangled with non-believers. Examples are Esau, the Israelite men and Moabite women during the time of Balak and Balaam (Num. 22–24), Samson, and Solomon.
Ahab ruled twenty-two years.	Why do the wicked sometimes seem to thrive so long?
Ahab, seventh king, son of wicked Omri makes it a goal to outdo Jeroboam (first northern kingdom king) in wickedness.	1 Peter 5:8a Be sober, be vigilant because your adversary, the devil, walks about like a roaring lion. (NKJV)
Jezebel leads Ahab and Israel into Baal worship.	Marrying an unbeliever—the chicken or the egg syndrome?
Ahab builds an altar and temple to Baal in Samaria, the city Omri had built.	Taking wickedness and future punishment from God to new levels.
Ahab also erected Asherah poles. The goddess Asherah was the consort of the pagan god El. The poles were probably wooden representations of Asherah.	Monuments to wickedness: the "Abomination that causes desolation (2 Thess. 2:3–4; Rev. 13:14ff). Any monuments being set up today?

Event	Message/Association
Ahab allowed the walls of Jericho (and its gates) to be rebuilt, against God's wishes.	Sins of omission: Authority figures not controlling lawlessness. Examples are Eli and sons, Hophni and Phinehas; our state and national government and leaders allowing gay marriage and promoting federally funded abortions.
Elijah proclaims to Ahab: No rain for three years because of his sins (1 Kings 17:1).	Ironic, in that the Canaanites said Baal was a fertility and rainfall god. Baal (who didn't really exist except in the minds of his idolatrous worshipers) was powerless to stop this curse.
God uses ravens, to feed his prophet east of the Jordan.	Someone has said this is the only known time that God used animals to feed the crown of his creation—man. God provides for those who love and worship Him, even in the darkest of times. What are some such times in your life?

Event	Message/Association
The miracle provision for the widow of Zarephath.	Others can receive vicarious blessing through their association with God's people. Examples: Salvation for an unbelieving spouse; blessings for our nation through friendship with Israel; the kings saved by Abraham during the rescue of Lot; Rahab, the prostitute.
Rising from the dead, the widow of Zarephath's son.	A foreshadowing of Jesus's and his disciples' power (from the Spirit) over death (to show the world, once and for all that we too will rise and be with Christ).
Obadiah becomes Elijah's messenger and the savior of one hundred of Yahweh's prophets (a Biblical "Schindler" who hid the godly men in caves, to save them from Ahab and Jezebel).	*Obadiah* means "servant of the Lord." The prophet Obadiah preached against people who rejoice in the misery of God's people. This Obadiah took a much bigger step of actually saving lives. "Even so faith, if it hath not works is dead" (James 1:17).

Event	Message/Association
Elijah defeats, then puts to death, 850 of Jezebel's wicked prophets: of Baal and Asherah (recalling the punishment of God through Moses of those who opposed God and Moses at Mt. Sinai).	Sometimes God's judgments are immediate. Recall Korah's rebellion; the leprosy upon Miriam, sister of Moses, or that on Uzziah; a bit slower than we would hope for, but a victory for believers and God at the end of times, nevertheless (Rev. 19:17–21).
Elijah hears the "sound of a heavy rain" (1 Kings 18:41, NIV): Ahab is notified.	Supernatural powers, special abilities are sometimes gifts to His children who surrender to Him: Examples would be the New Testament apostles as described in the book of Acts.

More Elijah Events

Elijah flees from Jezreel to Horeb: Jezreel in the north to Beersheba, first, in Judah. Along the way, "angel" feeds him twice (many believe it was a theophany). Then he goes to Horeb, probably Mt. Sinai, site of God's covenant, 250 miles further south, forty days and nights on two meals.	If you decide to go somewhere God did not plan, he may decide to send you even further to show you who is really in control.

Elijah's cave experience—a prime teaching moment. "What are you doing?" God asks the prophet. It was not God's command that he go here. "WEF" ("FEW" backward): a wind, earthquake, then fire pass by the prophet. God is in none of these. Instead, He's in a still small voice. Elijah had wanted to die. El Shaddai gives him new hope, new direction.

This is Elijah's new three-fold ministry:

1) Anoint Hazael king of Aram;
2) Anoint Jehu king of Israel;[2]
3) Anoint then train Elisha to succeed him as prophet (1 Kings 19:19).

Elijah pronounces a curse upon Ahab and his house (for the killing of Naboth; 1 Kings 21:17).

What prime teaching moments has God given you? (For example, a time when He really had your attention.) In my case, it was the end of a relationship. The relationship had led me away from Him. The end of it brought me back to Him.

Seek the still small voice of the Lord in all humility, and he will anoint your life with new direction and purpose.

God seeing wicked King Ahab's momentary repentance has some mercy upon him—raises a question: We will almost certainly see someone in heaven we never expected to see (not Ahab, though), like Manasseh?

By the Way

Elisha actually ended up anointing Jehu and Hazael, two out of the three final missions God gave to Elijah. Since Elisha was God's and, therefore, Elijah's chosen successor, he was deemed qualified to carry out these tasks. A modern example would be a lame duck president runs out of time in passing a favorite bill; an incoming president of the same party gets the bill passed.

On a different note, God sometimes uses His enemies to effect punishment on His way ward people. Hazael killed off Ahab's family, which is why God wanted him anointed as king by Elijah. Later, Hazael became an enemy of Israel. In more recent times, God helped the allies win WWII, using Russia to help punish the Nazis and take down that evil regime. Later, Russia became an enemy of the United States and of the entire free world.

Three-Point Comparison: Elijah, Revelation, and Application

Elijah	Revelation	Application
1 Kings 17:1–6	Revelation 1:9–11; 4:1–2	Be fearless in claiming God's word.
Elijah pronounces God's curse of famine upon the land due to Ahab and Jezebel. Elijah must flee for his life.	Rome banished John to the Patmos for proclaiming proclaiming Christ crucified.	
I Kings 16:29 ff	Revelation 2:20–23	In a democracy, we have a say in electing representatives and leaders who fear and love God, not people who will lead us into wickedness.
Ahab comes to power and quickly establishes himself as the most wicked king of all time.	Among the letters to the seven churches is one to Thyatira, a church that is allowing a New Testament Jezebel to corrupt the believers; the yeast is leavening the whole lump.	

Elijah	Revelation	Application
1 Kings 17:7–24	Revelation 3:7–8	God blesses those who wait upon the Lord: "But they that wait upon the Lord shall renew their strength" (Isa. 40:31).
The Widow of Zarephath: God's provision and miracle of resurrection to life for her son.	Blessings for Philadelphia, the virtuous church.	
1 Kings 18:2–4	Revelation 7:1–4	In times of spiritual and even actual war, God will protect His people.
The servant Obadiah—a Biblical Schindler.	God seals for eternity in His kingdom those who overcome.	

Elijah	Revelation	Application
1 Kings 18:16–40 The Mt. Carmel standoff between God's prophet, Elijah, and the 850 false prophets of Baal and Asherah: "You troubler of Israel" (Ahab to Elijah, upon their meeting).	Revelation 19:11–21 The Lamb, on a white horse, leading the armies of Heaven defeats the "beast" and his armies, sending the beast and the false prophet (two members of the evil trinity) to the lake of Fire.	Wickedness will be judged, and God's desire for His people will prevail.
1 Kings 19:9–18 The Mt. Horeb's (probably Mt. Sinai) appearance of God, before Elijah in the cave.	Revelation 21:3 "The tabernacle of God is with men" (NKJV).	"In Thee, oh Lord, do I put my trust" (Ps. 71:1a, KJV).
1 Kings 21:17–29 A curse upon the house of Ahab.	Revelation 20:9–10 Satan is defeated and cast into the lake of fire after the thousand-year reign of Christ.	God's people take comfort in knowing who will win.

Elijah	Revelation	Application
2 Kings 2:1–12 Elijah is raptured to heaven in a fiery chariot pulled by a fiery horse.	Revelation 4:1–5 John is taken into the throne room of heaven in a vision.	Be ready for God. Prepare your heart: "The day of the Lord will come just like a thief in the night" (1 Thess. 5:2, NASB).

Questions for Study

Challenge yourself to answer.

1. What does the name *Elijah* mean? (God is good/The Lord is my God) _____ _____

2. In what century BC did Elijah live? (Tenth/Ninth) ___ _____

3. In what two books of the Bible do we find Elijah's story? (1 and 2 Samuel/ 1 and 2 Kings) _____ and _____

4. Where can we find a statue of Elijah today? (Mt. Gerizim/Mt. Carmel) _____ _____

5. Thought question (no correct answer): What do you think was Elijah's finest hour? Your finest hour, by God's grace?_____

_____

The Relevance of Elijah Today

Dr. David Hocking speaks about the end of times and teaches others almost as regularly as you and I breathe, that we are not going to know who the antichrist is since God will rapture Christians before He reveals this secret.[4]

When God, therefore, raptured Elijah and we read and discuss this, we should feel warmed by the fire of that fiery chariot. Be warmed not like Peter was that night during the Lord's passion around the fire when the fisherman denied knowing Jesus three times (as Jesus, the Prophet and Son of God, had predicted he would). Be warmed, instead, by a fire of faith such as protected Shadrach, Meshach, and Abednego from Nebuchadnezzar's fiery furnace.

When the Lord's prophet (Elijah) stood on Mount Carmel, challenged, defeated, then killed the 850 false prophets, he was a prefigurement of what is going to happen at the culmination of the seven-year tribulation period. In Revelation 19:11, "Faithful and True" (πιστός και αληθινός) comes bursting out of the opened heavens, riding a white horse, eyes flashing like fire, leading the armies of heaven. It is the end for the enemy.

Dr. Hocking, finally, points out that we find the term *Lord of the Sabbath* 245 times in the Bible, and it is Jesus who is leading the armies of angels at the end of times. Jewish people, however, do not understand this. Some zealous Jews are gathering materials to rebuild the temple in Jerusalem. Yet Scripture says Jesus is the One who will do that, so they must be performing an exercise in futility.[5]

Elijah

Elijah never wrote
God's word of prophecy
And yet he stands a giant
With God-breathed legacy.

The feats our Lord accomplished
In Elijah's ministry
Have left a panorama
In Bible history:

James five and seventeen
Recalls the time he prayed
That God withhold the rain.
Three years, six months it stayed
Away. However, when he prayed again
It rained and rained and rained.

Widow at Zarephath:
Provisions and a life,
Footrace down Mt. Carmel
To mark the end of strife.

Two sets of fifty
Prophets marked for slaughter
Preserved in separate caves
By Obadiah, a godly "Schindler."[6]

Standoff with the prophets
Of Asherah and Baal—
Their God powerless,
Set up by God to fail.

Offering, wood, stones
Dust, trench, and water
Gone. Can you hear the prophets' groans
After Elijah's prayer?

Israel could not believe their eyes.
Down on the ground:
"The Lord, he is God"
From fear and wonder, their cries!

The prophets he seized,
At the Kishon Brook, slain.
Deuteronomy thirteen: thirteen[7]
Justified their death: it is plain.

When Ahab told his wife
All that Elijah did
She swore to take his life.
That is why he ran and hid.

Elijah, while in flight
Was serviced by the Lord.
Bread cakes baked on stones
"Arise, eat," twice, the word.

On Horeb in a cave
El Shaddai passed by his man
Not wind, earthquake, or fire
But a whisper, a voice, that ran

Something like this:
"Why are you here?"[8]
The people have missed
The mark. It is clear:

"No altars, broken covenant,
Prophets all slain.
Hear my rant—
I alone remain."

I have tasks for you:[9]
"Travel toward Damascus;
Anoint Hazael, king of Aram
Then for Israel I choose Jehu."

"Anoint Elisha next,
As prophet. Heed my call.
Seven thousand yet
Have kept themselves from Baal."

Other stories follow,
The Lord behind the scenes:
A victory for Ahab;
A chance to be brought low?

But no. He is not the Lord's, you know.
Micaiah comes with words from God
Speaking lies at first, but Ahab knows:
The vision? Defeat and death.

And so it goes:
In Israel Jehu reigned,
Jehoshaphat in Judah.
Naboth's blood avenged.

Two sets of fifty
Soldiers from Ahaziah
Received a death by fire.
No harm done to Elijah.

Then came the glorious end:
Elijah would not see death.
When God thought to send
A chariot of fire, it takes away our breath!

Notes

1. *Nelson's Compact Bible Dictionary*, 198–199
2. Ibid., 199
3. NASB Study Bible (Zondervan Publishing House, 1995), 489 notes how the anointings were merely to "designate as divinely appointed." In addition, Elisha, not Elijah, would complete the assignment of these anointings. Elijah and Elisha thus repeat the history of Moses and Joshua in the sense of one man receives a task and someone anoints the successor to complete that task.
4. Dr. David Hocking, speaking at the Great Lakes Prophecy Conference, Calvary Chapel, Appleton, Wisconsin, Saturday, September 7, 2013. Dr. Hocking's topic: "Can Israel survive current negotiations?"
5. Ibid.
6. "Oskar Schindler was an ethnic German industrial- ist, German spy, and member of the Nazi Party who is credited with saving the lives of 1,200 Jews during the Holocaust by employing them in his enamelware and ammunitions factories, which were located in occupied Poland and the Czech Republic," Wikipedia—the free online encyclopedia.
7. Actually, Deuteronomy 13:13–15 ff gives the full expla- nation for why God must deal a blow of the severest

nature to heathens and enticers to sin. They represent in many ways Satan's best shot at bringing down God's people. The theology seems to be to strike them down before they do the same to you. Spiritual warfare, perhaps especially in the Old Testament, justifies actual physical warfare.

8. God is speaking here, the beginning of a dialogue now between the Lord and his prophet.
9. The Lord is speaking now.

Elijah placed his cloak upon Elisha,
symbolizing God's choice for prophetic succession.

Elisha

אלישע על רוח אליהו נחה ויאמרו־

They [the sons of the prophets who were at Jericho] said: "The spirit of Elijah rests on Elisha."

—2 Kings 2:15b (NASB)

ELISHA MEANS "MY God saves" (in contrast with *Elijah*, "the Lord is my God"). Elisha served for about fifty years in the northern kingdom, succeeding his mentor, Elijah. Kings Elisha served under included Jehoram, Jehu, Jehoahaz, and Joash roughly during the years 850–800 BC. We first hear of Elisha in 1 Kings 19:16 where the Lord mentioned, during the Mount Horeb cave encounter, Elijah's anointing of Elisha as one of the former's three major upcoming responsibilities. We learn the rest of his story in 2 Kings. Among the tasks assigned by the Lord to His servant included

anointing and advising kings, a ministry of helps and evangelism to the needy, accentuated by a divine appointment
to perform several miracles throughout the course of his
lifetime of service to the Lord.

Before Elijah left this earth in a dramatic rapture via
a fiery chariot, he asked Elisha what blessing he would
like to receive. Elisha, by his answer, showed his servant's
heart. Instead of worldly gain (of which Elijah had none),
he requested a double portion of his master's prophetic
gifts. In so doing, he was also asking for the firstborn son's
inheritance (since Elisha was like a son to Elijah). Elijah
responded with something interesting if not puzzling.
Elijah told his pupil he might receive this gift if he were
present at the moment of Elijah's rapture. Elisha proved
his tenacity by sticking to Elijah like a fly on flypaper.
Elisha's determination is not unlike the passion of Jacob
during his wrestling match with an angel, refusing to let go
until he got his blessing. This final challenge would prove
to be God's and Elijah's last lesson for the chosen successor. Elisha shows himself worthy of his calling, never losing
sight of Elijah. Most importantly, later on as well, he never
lost sight of God nor of the Lord's will for his life.

When I think of both Elijah and Elisha, I see two great
men of God who were not only called upon to prophesy
but were rewarded for their faithful service and moral
leadership by being allowed to share in the performance

of miracles like our Lord and Savior, Jesus, performed. In a sense, therefore, they foreshadowed Jesus. The difference was Jesus was the Son of God showing His divinity through marvelous miracles while humbly clothed in humanity. Elijah and Elisha, instead, as James says (about Elijah), were mere men, serving the Lord, but blessed with experiencing divine acts as a reward for their faithfulness in pointing to the true Messiah to come (James 5:17).

Points of Interest

Schools of prophets had grown up in the wake of the great prophet, priest, and judge, Samuel. Of Bethel, Gilgal, and Mizpah, the three main cities in the itinerant judge's circuit, two—Bethel and Gilgal (along with Jericho)—had become centers of prophetic training by the time of Elijah and Elisha. This becomes evident in the account of Elijah's last day on earth: He visits two of the three places as one of his last acts. Elisha witnesses the departure and presumably receives the blessing he had requested. This theory can be tested and confirmed by taking into account the number of amazing things God accomplished through Elisha during the fifty-year course of his ministry.

Going back to his early calling, that Elisha came from a wealthy family was shown by the fact that Elijah found him plowing with twelve yoke of oxen (we find this story in 1

Kings 19:19–21). Apparently, the extensive fields consisted of twelve sections. Elisha was working one of the twelve when God, through Elijah, came calling. One symbolic act that inaugurated the beginning of Elisha's ministry was Elijah's throwing of his cloak over the shoulders of Elisha as he greeted him in the field that eventful day. This same cloak was the one used by both Elijah on his last day and Elisha, on his first day as God's prophet, to part the waters of the Jordan River. This act signified the passing of the torch of prophecy to a new generation. It would be years before God would actually call Elijah home. Meanwhile, Elisha began training for service to God.

Ahaziah (ruled from 853–852 BC), Ahab's son, evil like his parents, died as prophesied shortly after becoming king. Like father, like son, as far as the evil they were devoted to. Yet Ahaziah, unlike father Ahab, ruled only one year instead of his father's twenty-two years. This seems more like the poetic justice we would hope for from a just God (as we perceive justice, through our dim glass vision—as Paul states so eloquently, through the Spirit's inspiration, in 1 Corinthians 13:12).

Elisha seemed a bit eccentric when performing his prophetic wonders, on more than one occasion. In 2 Kings 3:14–16, for example, music accompanied the prophetic power that came over him (an association that seems to have been a part of the training going on at the schools of the prophets since the time of Samuel). Under the inspiration and influence of this preparation, God gave him a vision to order a valley dug full of ditches so that the divine provision of victory from the Moabite menace could occur the next day.

In 2 Kings 6:8–10, we discover that God has granted Elisha the miracle gift of being a fly on the wall in the war conference room of the King of Syria.[1]

God tells Elisha on several occasions when and where the Syrians are planning to strike, thus foiling their plans and saving the day for God's people. A Syrian spy eventually reveals this gift to the Syrian king, leading to the king placing a price upon the prophet's head. Eventually, a Syrian army surrounds him, which leads to another miracle. The army of angels that, in turn, surrounded the Syrian army is followed by the latter's being blinded to a man. Later, God's people mercifully give their enemy a meal and send them home, which led to peace between the two foes for a generation. God took a plan of the enemy and turned it into an opportunity to reveal His power and glory. How often do we see that occurring in Scripture? How often in our own lives?

Miracles of Elijah and Elisha Compared[2]

Elijah	Elisha
1. Kept the widow, her son, and himself alive by divine provision.	1. Uses Elijah's cloak to part the waters of the Jordan.
2. Raises the widow's son to life.	2. Using salt in a bowl, he pours it into a local spring that had been contaminated. This purifies the waters. Amazing miracle through odd means (2 Kings 2:21–23).
3. Defeated the prophets of Baal and Asherah (1 Kings 18:20–46)	3. Idolatrous, mocking young men or boys killed by two bears, toward Bethel, for calling Elisha "Old Baldy" (after the indignant prophet calls down a curse upon their heads).
4. Supernatural race from Mt. Carmel to Jezreel (nineteen miles)	4. Under the anointed playing of a minstrel, God devises a plan to save Israel from a Moabite attack involving ditches, water, and sunlight (2 Kings 3:15–25).

Elijah	Elisha
5. He was ministered to (in a theophany, some believe, by Jesus); fed twice, he survived Jezebel's henchmen. Here, a miracle was done for him rather than God doing a miracle through him.	5. Helps a woman avoid selling her sons to pay off a debt. God, through the instructions of His prophet, provides a continuous product of oil borrowed from neighbors. She then sells this oil to pay off the debt.
6. Kills off by fire two sets of fifty henchmen sent by King Ahaziah.	6. The Lord, through Elisha, provides a son for a previously barren Shunammite woman.
7. Parted the waters of the Jordan using his cloak as a staff.	7. Brings the Shunammite boy back to life after he had died.
	8. Makes safe a poisonous stew of prophets' sons at Gilgal after adding flour to the pot.
	9. He multiplies bread.
	10. He heals Naaman, the leprosy-infected Syrian military commander.

Elijah	Elisha
	11. Curse for Gehazi, the greedy, covetous servant.
	12. God defies gravity through the miracle of the floating ax head. God gives proof of his sovereignty over his laws of nature.
	13. The Syrian army that had surrounded Elisha, God's fly on the Wall of Syrian military planners, is Itself surrounded, then blinded (reflecting their spiritual blindness). The subsequent journey to Samaria, the humiliation, where they were Fed and released, led to no immediate reprisals. God was offering them mercy and a chance at salvation, powerful enough to silence them for a long time, but not enough to convert them in large numbers like happened with Nineveh, during the ministry of Jonah, a few generations before Elijah (2 Kings 6:8–23 for this miracle story).

Elijah	Elisha

14. The king, speaking with Gehazi, servant of Elisha, wants to know details concerning the "great things" God has done through Elisha (2 Kings 8:4).

15. Toward the end of his life, he denounces Jehoash for his lack of full faith (as displayed in the weak manner of his striking the ground, responding to Elisha's command.) His victories, Elisha now proclaims, will be much fewer than they would have been otherwise (2 Kings 13:18).

16. Years after the death of Elisha, news comes of the miraculous restoration to life of a body tossed into the tomb of Elisha, having come into contact with Elisha's bones (2 Kings 13:20–21).

Three-Point Comparison: Elisha, Revelation, and Personal Application

Elisha	Revelation	Application
Elisha parts the Jordan with Elijah's miracle cloak.	Revelation 22:1 The river of the water of life (Ex. 14:21–2: Moses's parting of the Dead Sea brings life to God's people and death to God's enemies.)	This river will be part of the beauty of our new home; nothing shall be able to separate us from the love of Christ (Rom. 8:35).
Elisha purifies the polluted spring of water through Christ—an application of salt.	Revelation 8:10–11 and Revelation 21:6 Contrast between waters poisoned from wormwood and the water of life in heaven.	Drink from the water of life, Jesus, on a daily basis (read His word and live). Also, we are the salt of the earth (Matt. 5:13)—hope from God for the lost in the world.

Elisha	Revelation	Application
Forty-two young men threatening Elisha on his way to Bethel ("Go up, oh baldy") are killed by God-sent bears (2 Kings 2:23–25).	Revelation 6:17 For the great day of His wrath has come.	Proverbs 30:17 and Ephesians 6:1–3 Warnings to youth
When Elisha returned to Gilgal, there was a famine in the land (2 Kings 4:38).	"A quart of wheat for a denarius, and three quarts of barley for a denarius" (Rev. 6:6 (NASB) during the first wave of the tribulation, third seal—when food sold for an exorbitant price due to famine).	Christians will be reaching out in mercy to help those in famine—till the end of times. Spiritual famine calls for spiritual revival.

Questions for Review

Choose the correct answer.

1. What does *Elisha* mean? ("My God Saves"/"My God is great") _____

____

2. For about how many years did Elisha serve? (Ten/ Fifty) _____

3. What kingdom did Elijah serve? (Northern/ Southern) _____

4. What are roughly the years Elisha served? From (650–620/850–800) _____ to _____

5. What was Elijah doing when we first hear of Elisha? (Challenging wicked Queen Jezebel's priests/ Having an encounter with God in a cave) _____

_____

How Elisha Is Relevant for Christians Today

In 2 Kings 6:8–23, the story of God's protection of Elisha by surrounding the Syrian army with an army of angels, we have a foreshadowing of what will happen at the end of times when the Lamb, eyes flashing, comes to lead his armies against Satan. The outcome is swift and sure, ending with God throwing Satan into the lake of fire for an eternity.

The idea of an enemy hearing or knowing that we are on to them and then someone warning our people about them is nothing new to a modern Christian. Watchtower Christians (we might call them) are talking about heresy. Heresy, perhaps the most insidious of all enemies, involves, among other things, the invasion of false teachings creeping into our midst and threatening biblical truths.

Eric Barger, for example, is warning Christians all over America about the danger of liberalism. He points out that it is affecting Methodists, Presbyterians, the ELCA, some Mennonites, some Baptists (including American Baptists and Southern Baptists), just to name a few. He warns that it starts in seminaries where basic biblical doctrines come under attack. He reflects that the German Enlightenment, leading to textual criticism, begun some 150 years ago, was a powerful source of a movement away from Christ and the Bible.

From the seminaries, new pastors carry these ideas to their congregations. Heretic seminary professors, therefore, are an example of the potential armies of the enemy that we need to be on the lookout for.

Eric Barger would be our Elisha, our "fly on the wall" of the seminary classrooms who, with his ear to the ground, is on the alert for false teaching, ready to warn the rest of us regarding any possible infestation. Eric illustrates his concern with the words, "Bible believers define culture by the Bible; but liberals define the Bible by culture." He also argues that "corrupt Bibliology leads to corrupt theology, ending with corrupt Christology" (where even the virgin birth is being questioned). Yet the virgin birth makes all the difference in the world to our beliefs. Many of these heretics are even calling into question the bodily resurrection of Christ. Mr. Barger cites a recent poll that questioned 744. The results are alarming: 13 percent of American Lutheran pastors said they do not believe Jesus arose from the dead; 30 percent of Presbyterians said the same; 33 percent of American Baptists, 35 percent of Episcopalians, and a whopping 51 percent of Methodist ministers do not believe. Wolves posing as sheep or shepherds are leading the sheep astray.[5]

Elisha

"My God saves," Elijah's protégé
Was not unlike Solomon
For whom wisdom held sway:
For spiritual gifts he prayed.[6]

He sought twice Elijah's power.
So it was, Elisha saw the rapture
Of his master, Elijah—
Said gifts, then he captured.

"The spirit of Elijah rests on Elisha,"
Said prophets' sons at Jericho.
Just like Elijah's mantle, the spirit
Covered him head to toe.

The anointing he enjoyed,
The visions he received:
Like Moabite ditches dug
Snatching victory from defeat.

Young boys who came a mocking
"Old baldy, rise," they said.
His curse: to God, in talking.
Response? Two bears, boys dead.[7]

The widow of a prophet's son
With enslavement looming close[8]
And freedom all but done
Sought a remedy: Elisha she chose.

A jar of oil, other jars too
(Borrowed from neighbors
As neighbors often do)
Led to a business in oils.

Her worries were through!
Poisonous gourds, Elisha's next case—
Accidentally put into the stew.
"Add some flour" (which made it safe!).

Elijah raised a Zarephite son.
Elisha, in turn—a Shunammite one.
Elijah's needs, a personal gift.
Elisha's bread, a hundred fed:

Feeding a hundred with five loaves
Foreshadowed the miracle of Christ
Where, for the latter, they'd come in droves
To receive the bread of life.

A little Israelite maid,
A servant in Naaman's home, his domain,
Was used by a sovereign lord
To bring healing and god to an Aramean.[9]

In building a house by the Jordan
The prophets' sons had a mishap
A borrowed ax head fell in
Gravity defied! A stick thrown in. It came up![10]

Syrians one day heard
That he, their plans foreknew.
This news left them perturbed,
Then surrounded, blinded, blue.

Jeremiah had his Baruch.
Elisha had Gehazi—
Assistants who served a prophet
Usually in a way *sehr gut*.[11]

Notes

1. NASB Study Bible (Zondervan Publishing House, 1995),
    506, says the Aramean king was "probably Ben-hadad II."
2. The comparison is in, roughly, chronological order
3. Some interesting parallels occur here to events involv-
    ing Jesus and his disciples: First, in 2 Kings 4:27 we
    hear how the Shunammite woman came looking for
    Elisha, trusting he could raise her son. The prophet
    pushes her away first, however. Jesus's disciples at times
    had the effrontery to speak for the Lord, being on the
    verge of sending someone away, but Jesus attended to
    the needs requested. Elisha and Gehazi, thus, function
    as Old Testament types of the Savior and his disciples.
    In addition when the Shunammite, in 2 Kings 4:30,
    refuses to leave Elisha until he has attended to her
    son, she unwittingly mirrors the actions of Elisha at
    the pending rapture of Elijah—the protégé who also
    would not leave his master's presence up to the very
    end. Another parallel, Jacob, in wrestling with the angel
    (Gen. 32:26) and vowing to not let go "unless you bless
    me" (NASB). All of these examples show that we can be
    tenacious with God, in his face, if you will, yet hum-
    bly seeking his blessings. What a powerful example of
    faith for us all! God wants us to emulate these exam-
    ples, I believe.

4. In ancient schools of rhetoric, a popular literary trope involved starting your speech noting all the accomplishments you could mention, but due to time constraints, the speaker chooses to "pass over." Hence, the name for this trope, *praeteritio*, which, in Greek, means to "pass over." Here God gives a visual demonstration of His sovereignty over the natural world—fire, earthquake, and wind—then proceeds to pass over these demonstrations of power to focus on his chosen method of communication for the moment—a quiet voice (not unlike the conscience God has placed in each of us, reminding us of our responsibilities at times of hesitation).

5. Eric Barger, speaker during session 10 at the Great Lakes Prophecy Conference, Calvary Chapel, Appleton, Wisconsin, Saturday, September 7, 2013.

6. Elisha prayed for more powers even than God had given Elijah.

7. We hear this account in 2 Kings 2:23 ff.

8. Exodus 21:1–2 allowed temporary enslavement for debt. In this case, a cruel creditor was about to take the widow's sons from her.

9. Washing in the Jordan River seven times cured him of his leprosy, an instruction that first challenged his pride and then humbled him in preparation for receiving grace and mercy from the one true God. We learn this story in 2 Kings 5.

10. Have you ever noticed that fanciful instructions at times accompany miracles performed through the prophets (2 Kings 6:1–7)? "Here, throw a stick in the water where the ax head fell in." To Naaman the prophet said, "Wash yourself seven times in the Jordan." Such miracles, then, appear to be types of the miracles Jesus performed (like healing the blind man by spitting in a handful of dirt, then rubbing it on the man's eyes, then having him wash it off in the Pool of Siloam in Jerusalem—as told in John 9:1–6 ff.)

11. *Sehr gut* is German for "very good." Unfortunately, 2 Kings 5:15 ff describes a moment of greed for Gehazi, Elisha's helper, and the resultant punishment of leprosy for him and his descendants.

[note to layout: insert photo 4; centralize]

Isaiah, undoubtedly the greatest of the writing prophets—
receives his vision from the Lord and faithfully
records all for posterity, in service to His Lord.

Isaiah

בשנת־מות המלך עזיהו ואראה את־אדני ישב על כסא רם ונשא

In the year of King Uzziah's death, I saw the
Lord seated on a throne lofty and exalted.

—Isaiah 6:1 (NASB)

Notes on the Prophet Isaiah

MANY CALL ISAIAH, son of Amoz, the greatest of the writing prophets. (Elijah and Elisha were not writing prophets) His name means "the Lord saves." A contemporary of Amos, Hosea, and Micah, his service began in 740 BC at the death of King Uzziah.[1]

His ministry extended through the reigns of five different kings until at least 701 BC (Isaiah 37–39—the historical interlude ending with the reign of good king Hezekiah, just prior to that of wicked Manasseh) or possibly to about 681 BC.

"The Ascension of Isaiah", from Jewish tradition, says wicked King Manasseh placed Isaiah in a hollow tree trunk and then had him sawn in half (Tradition says he later repented while captive in Babylon).[2] Mentioned in Hebrews 11:37 of a martyr who died this way may refer to Isaiah.

There are those who historically have challenged Isaiah's authorship of the entire book under his name. Arguments for the unity of Isaiah, to the contrary, (his authorship of all sixty-six chapters) include his expression "the Holy One of Israel," which occurs twelve times in chapters 1–39 and fourteen times in chapters 40–66. Outside of Isaiah, it only appears six more times in the OT. Some have argued there are two authors (at the divisions mentioned) and some argue for three. Isaiah's is the only name attached to the book, however (at 1:1, 2:1, and 13:1). He may have written 1–39 in his earlier ministry (culminating in the fall of Assyria in 701 BC). The other half (40–66) may have been written afterward (between 701 and 681.) We know he was still alive in 681 BC. Many credit Isaiah with writing the history of King Uzziah also, found in 2 Chronicles 26.[3]

That a prophet may have written one of the prosaic and historical books (like part of 2 Chronicles) is in line with the belief by many, for instance, that a prophet (ancient Jewish tradition said it was Jeremiah) wrote the conclusion to David's reign as told in 1 Kings 2:1–4.[4]

Jesus quoted more extensively from Isaiah than any other prophet. Prophetic utterances, not therefore uncoinicidentally, referring to the Savior also abound in this greatly anointed man of God, more so, in fact, than in any other Old Testament prophet. This reciprocal connection between Jesus and His prophet strongly suggests the bond of a personal relationship, the likes of which we all seek on a daily basis today. The blessings of fellowship with Jesus will last into eternity. If it is true Isaiah suffered a martyr's death, we can expect to see him in the throne room of heaven with extra crowns of honor—rewards for being faithful unto death. (As Revelation 2:10b [KJV] says, in the letter to Smyrna, "Be thou faithful unto death, and I will give thee the crown of life.")

Famous Passages

> "Come now let us reason together," says the Lord; "though your sins are as scarlet they shall be white as snow. Though they be red like crimson, they shall be as wool." [The blood of Christ cleanses us from all evil.] (Isa. 1:18)

I am ruined, for I am a man of unclean lips and I live among a people of unclean lips; for my eyes have seen the King, the Lord of hosts. (Isa. 6:5)

Then I heard the voice of the Lord saying, "Whom shall I send, and who will go for us? Then I said 'Here am I. Send me.'" [The response should be immediate availability, as a bondservant to the master, when the Lord calls upon us to serve him and his interests in the world.] (Isa. 6:8)

For to us a child is born, to us a son is given, and the government shall be upon his shoulders [heard at Christmastime yearly]. (Is. 9:6a, ESV)

A voice of one calling in the desert prepare the way for the Lord. Make straight in the desert a highway for our God [quoted by John the Baptist at the beginning of his ministry—eg, Matt. 3:1–3]. (Isa. 40:3, NIV)

The flower fades but the word of our God stands forever. [God's unchanging nature—a message modern Christians need to remember as we weather the storms of our pagan contemporaries who think removing God from public dialogue will push him out of existence, out of sight, out of mind!] (Isa. 40:8, NASB)

Who has directed the spirit of the Lord, or as his counselor has informed him? [Deep humility at realization of the sovereignty of the Lord, quoted by Paul at Romans 11:34.] (Isa. 40:13, NASB)

Fear not for I am with you; be not dismayed for I am your God. I will strengthen you. I will help you; I will uphold you with my righteous right hand. [Encouragement to stay the battle and hold on to our faith despite the forces arrayed against us.] (Isa. 41:10, ESV)

A bruised reed he will not break and a smoldering wick he will not snuff out. [Jesus, to those who love him, will become the still small voice, the barely perceptible breeze that Elijah experienced, in a moment of trepidation, at the cave on Mt. Horeb. Contrast this gentleness with the strong wind, earthquake, and fire, which God chooses not to frighten us with, when we seek him.] (Isa. 42:3a, NIV)

I am the Lord. That is my name. I will not give my glory to another nor my praise to graven images

[God's promise to enforce the first commandment against idolatry]. (Isa. 42:8, NASB)

I, even I, am the Lord and there is no savior besides me, a reminder to a people prone to fall for the polytheism so rampant around them. [Also, the jealous and sovereign God idea is expressed mightily in Psalm 46:10b: "I will be exalted among the nations. I will be exalted in the earth."] (Isa. 43:11, NASB)

Will the clay say to the potter, "What are you doing?" Or the thing you are making say, "He has no hands"? [A warning against spiritual pride.] (Is. 45:9b, NASB)[5]

Thus says the Lord to Cyrus His anointed whom I have taken by the right hand to subdue nations before him [a miraculous and breathtakingly accurate, down to even the exact name, prediction of the pagan emperor who some one hundred and fifty to two hundred years later would free the captive children of Abraham from the hands of Babylonian oppression]. (Isa. 45:1a, NASB)

How beautiful on the mountains are the feet of those who bring good news. [Here is an encouragement for any evangelist or preacher of the truth, whether he or she be famous, or just an obscure sidewalk Christian warrior! Paul quotes this in Romans 10:15.] (Isa. 52:7a, NIV)

(The prophet uses the next five passages powerfully to evoke images of the Passion during Lent and Passion Week. Some have been the inspiration for Christian hymns and songs throughout the centuries)[6]

He was despised and forsaken of men, a man of sorrows and acquainted with grief. (Isa. 53:3a, NASB)

Surely he hath borne our griefs and carried our sorrows. Yet did we did esteem him stricken, smitten of God, and afflicted. (Isa. 53:4, KJV)

But he was pierced for our transgressions. He was crushed for our iniquities. The punishment that brought us peace was upon him and by his wounds, we are healed. (Isa. 53:5, NIV)

All we like sheep have gone astray; we have turned every one to his own way; and the LORD hath laid on him the iniquity of us all. (Isa. 53:6, KJV)

He was oppressed and He was afflicted, Yet he did not open his mouth; Like a lamb that is led to slaughter, and like a sheep that is silent before its shearers, so he did not open his mouth. (Isa. 53:7b, NASB)

For the mountains shall depart, and the hills be removed; but my kindness shall not depart from thee, neither shall the covenant of my peace be removed, saith the LORD that hath mercy on thee. [Sounds like the prophet revealing his acquaintance with Psalm 46:2. Also, these are great words of comfort for those who otherwise might fear a righteous avenging God]. (Is.54:10a, KJV)

Seek the Lord while he may be found; call on him while he is near. (Isa. 55:6, NASB)

For my thoughts are not your thoughts, nor are your ways my ways declares the Lord [this thought was expanded upon by the Apostle Paul in 1 Corinthians 2:9: "Eye has not seen, nor ear heard"]. (Isa. 55:8, NASB)

So is my word that goes forth out from my mouth. It will not return unto me empty [used by the Gideons as their signature verse]. (Isa. 55:11a, NIV)

"There is no peace," says my God, "for the wicked." (Isa. 57:21, NASB)

Their feet rush into sin. They are swift to shed innocent blood. (Isa. 59:7a, NIV)

For the nation and the kingdom which will not serve you will perish. (Isa. 60:12, NASB)

Famous Passages continued...

The spirit of the Lord God is upon me because the Lord has anointed me to bring good news to the afflicted. (Is.61:1, NASB) [Jesus, our Savior, quoted this verse while teaching in the temple in Nazareth one day, shortly after the three-fold temptation in the wilderness at the beginning of his ministry as told in Luke 4:18–19. He punctuated it with, "Today this Scripture has been fulfilled in your hearing" (Luke 4:21, NASB). Shortly after this, he was run out of town with enemies intending to throw him over a cliff, having accused him of blasphemy (Luke 4:28–30). His suffering and rejection had begun. Hebrews instructs us that the word is sharper than any two-edged sword. When prophets reminded people of their ancestors' sins and the people understood the Lord's comparison to them, they could not endure it. The same reaction occurred later, in the early church, after Stephen uttered a similar rebuke. Paul also experienced this. Others who heard the good news, on the other hand, would respond differently, crying out in despair: What must I do to be saved? (Acts 16:30). Thank God for the latter, revealing their open minds and broken, repentant hearts.] (Isa. 61:1a)

For all of us have become like one who is unclean, and all our righteous deeds are like a filthy garment. (Isa. 64:6a, NASB)

For behold I will create new heavens and a new earth; and the former things will not be remembered or come to mind. (Isa. 65:17, NASB)

Thus says the Lord, "Heaven is my throne and the earth is my footstool." (Isa. 66:1a, NASB)

Reasons for the Hebrews' Fall from Grace

As you read and meditate on these verses, ask yourself if your country has not fallen to a certain extent in some, if not all, of these areas. If that is the case, let us pray together for a rebirth of freedom for your country. Freedom is a word we all understand. Adults taught us to cherish it since we were toddlers on our grandparents' knees. Even deeper and more urgent is the need to receive God's freedom from sin and the devil that comes through fellowship with and obedience to our triune God—Father, Son (Jesus Christ), and Holy Spirit. Which of these accusations can we apply to your nation, to our nation, to other so-called Christian nations around the world today?

Your rulers are rebels and companions of thieves [like Pottersville in *It's a Wonderful Life*]. (Isa. 1:23)

Not bringing offerings [In many church denominations today, pastors are afraid to speak of the tithe for fear of losing members]. (Isa. 43:22–23)

None [no sons] to guide Israel. (Isa. 51:18)

Going through the ritual motions of worship, yet not treating people with love and justice. (Isa. 58:2–5)

Israel did not answer God's call; God spoke; they did not listen; they did evil in God's sight [In Psalm 46:6, when God spoke, "the earth melted." There followed a description of the mighty power of God unleashed upon a spiritually deaf and dead world. God's power can devastate or it can make wars to cease from one end of the earth to the other. He reserves a better outcome for those who listen when he speaks]. (Isa. 65:11–12)

How Can God Be an Author of Evil?

I have created the waster to destroy.[7] (Isa. 54:16b, KJV)

Promises of Blessing for the Righteous

In the future he will honor Galilee of the Gentiles [through Jesus]. (Isa. 9:1)

The desert and the parched land will be glad: The wilderness will rejoice and blossom [the modern state of Israel can boast fulfillment of this prophecy]. (Isa. 35:1a, NIV)

King Hezekiah's song of praise to God who gave him 15 more years of life after his lament to God who was about to take his life.[8] (Isa. 38:9–22)

I will make rivers flow. (Isa. 41:18a, NIV)

Sing to the Lord a new song [we should always have a song on our lips and in our hearts, dedicated in service to Christ]. (Isa. 42:10a, NIV)

For I will pour water on the thirsty land [this would be good news for any place experiencing drought—true in a figurative, spiritual sense, as well—a place where the Lord's will has not been sought out in a long time]. (Isa. 44:3a, NASB)

I have wiped out your transgressions like a thick cloud. [an answer to the psalmist's prayer in Psalm 130:8—"He...will redeem Israel from all their sins."]. (Isa. 44:22a, NASB)

Listen to me, you who pursue righteousness who seek the Lord [the Lord will both protect and reward the righteous, those seeking maturity and growth in their faith]. (Isa. 51:1a, NASB)

Shout for joy, O barren one, you who have borne no child. (Isa. 54:1a, NASB)

"Come, all you who are thirsty, come to the waters" [the appeal during any evangelistic effort, large or small] (Isa. 55:1a). Jesus told the Samaritan woman at the well to drink of [Him] the "water that leads to eternal life" [paraphrased]. (John 4:14, NIV).

Thus says the LORD, "Preserve justice and do right-eousness" [pray our judges and legislators at all levels—local, state, and national—will return, in obedience, to this command]. (Isa. 56:1a, NASB)

You come to the help of those who gladly do right [more rewards for those seeking the Lord's heart]. (Isa. 64:5a, NIV)

There is no one who calls on your name [repeated by Paul in Romans 3:10–12]. (Isa. 64:7a, NASB)

Particularly Poignant Metaphors and Similes: Turns of Phrase Referring to God, His People, and Our Relationship with Him

The bill of your mother's divorcement. (Isa. 50:1)

My creditors [God "sold" his people to for their sins]. (Isa. 50:1)

Behold all ye that kindle a fire and compass yourselves about with sparks...ye shall lie down in sorrow [those who engage in sins before God and man;
if you make your own bed, you will sleep in it, as we
say sometimes]. (Isa. 50:11, KJV)

Look to the rock from which you were hewn, and to
the quarry from which you were dug.] (Isa. 51:1–2,
NASB)

And her [Zion's] wilderness he will make like Eden,
and her desert like the garden of the Lord. (Isa.
51:3b, NASB)

The chalice of my anger [is removed, as God seeks
to renew a loving relationship with us]. (Isa. 51:22b,
NASB)

Buy wine and milk without money and without cost
[blessings for the righteous]. (Isa. 55:1b, NASB)

Rhetorical Questions in Isaiah

Can a woman forget her nursing child? (Isa. 49:15,
NASB)

Is my hand shortened at all, that it cannot redeem? or have I no power to deliver? (Isa. 50:2, KJV)

Who will contend with me? Who is mine adversary? (Isa. 50:8b, KJV)

Who is he that condemns me? (Isa. 50:9, NASB)

But where is the fury of the oppressor? (Isa. 51:13, NASB)

By whom shall I comfort thee? (Isa. 51:19, KJV])

Four Servant (Jesus) Songs

He will bring forth justice to the Gentiles. (Isa. 42:1–9)

Thus says the Lord, the Redeemer of Israel. (Isa. 49:1–15)

I gave my back to those who strike me. (Isa. 50:6a, NASB)

But he was pierced through for our transgressions. He was crushed for our iniquities. (Isa. 53:5, NASB)

New Things Are Coming

Behold the former things have come to pass, now I declare new things [Jesus, in Mel Gibson's *The Passion*, speaks these words in a paraphrase to his mother, Mary, on the Via Dolorosa (on His way to the cross) in a scene that captured the moment's pathos]. (Isa. 42:9a, NASB)

References to Moses and the Israelites of the Torah

Generations of old. (Isa. 51:9)

Idea of a Remnant

Unless the Lord Almighty had left us some survivors we would be like Sodom. We would be like Gomorrah. (Isa. 1:9a, NASB)

Shear-jashub, son of Isaiah [his name means "a remnant shall return"]. (Isa. 7:3)

Once more a remnant of the house of Judah will take root [it is fair to assume any passage mentioning a remnant would involve a pun on the Hebrew word, calling to mind the name of the prophet's son]. (Isa.37:31a, NIV)

For out of Jerusalem will go forth a remnant and out of Mount Zion survivors. (Isa. 37:32a)

I will not destroy them all. (Isa. 65:8b, NIV)

Messianic Prophecies

Therefore the Lord himself shall give you a sign; Behold, a virgin shall conceive, and bear a son, and shall call his name Immanuel. [recited in children's services at Christmas time]. (Isa. 7:14, KJV)

For unto us a child is born, unto us a son is given: and the government shall be upon his shoulder. [also recited by children at Christmas time]. (Isa. 9:6a, KJV)

And He will be the stability of your times (Isa. 33:6a, NASB)

Behold, your God will come.... He will come and save you. (Isa. 35:4, KJV)

Then will the eyes of the blind be opened and the ears of the deaf will be unstopped. (Isa. 35:5a, NASB)

Say to the towns of Judah: "Here is your God." (Isa. 40:9b, NIV)

A bruised reed he [Jesus] will not break and a dimly burning wick he will not extinguish [He will have a gentle side to him]⁹ (Isa. 42:3a, NASB)

I gave my back to the smiters and my cheeks to them that plucked off the hair. (Isa. 50:6a, KJV)

Just as there were many who were appalled at him. (Isa. 52:14a, NIV)

He was despised and rejected of men, a man of sorrows, and acquainted with grief. (Isa. 53:3a, KJV)

A Redeemer will come to Zion. (Isa. 59:20a, NASB)

See your Savior comes [Matthew points out how Jesus's entry into Jerusalem riding on a donkey during Holy Week was another prophecy fulfillment]. (Isa. 62:11a, NIV)

Parallel Passages

Isaiah 2:3b

"That He may teach us concerning His ways And that we may walk in His paths." (NASB)

Matthew 7:13–14

"Enter through the narrow gate; for the gate is wide and the way is broad that leads to destruction, and there are many who enter through it." (NASB)

Isaiah 2:19a (NASB)

"Men will go to caves in the rocks and to holes of the ground" (sounds like the foxholes of WWI or the tunnel people of the Vietnam War)

Revelation 6:15–16 (NASB)

Then the kings of the earth and the great men and the commanders and the rich and the strong and every slave and free man hid themselves in the caves and among the rocks of the mountains.

Isaiah 52:7b (NASB)

"How lovely on the mountains are the feet of him who brings good news."

Luke 2:10b

"I bring you good news of great joy that will be for all the people."

Isaiah 52:15a (NASB)

"Thus he will sprinkle many nations."

Romans 15:21a

"Those who were not told about him will see."

Isaiah 54:11b (NASB)

Revelation 21:19

"And your foundations I will lay in sapphires [awaiting us in Heaven]."

"A foundation of sapphires [in Heaven, awaits us]."

Apocalyptic Passages in Isaiah

The heavens shall vanish away like smoke. (Isa. 51:6b, KJV)

Comparison: Isaiah, Revelation, and a Personal Application

Isaiah	Revelation	Application
Isaiah 6:1–3	Revelation 4	We too, one day, will be visitors to the throne room of God.
Isaiah visits the throne room of God.	John, in a vision, is called to the throne room of God.	
Isaiah 9:13	Revelation 9:20	Recalls Pharaoh at the time of Moses. Eventually what can happen is that God can harden your heart. You are headed, as we say, hell-bent on destruction—self-destruction.
Yet the people do not turn back to Him who struck them, Nor do they seek the LORD of hosts. (NASB)	Despite the punishment of the seven seals and six of the seven trumpets, the rest of mankind (not yet killed) still did not repent.	

Isaiah	Revelation	Application
Isaiah 9:14–15	Revelation 9:7, 10	Whether head or tail, those who torment others may have their way for a while as God's pawns. In the end, they will be destroyed.
The head and the tail: Head is the elders and prominent men. The tail is the false prophets.	The head and tail of the locusts, released with smoke, from the abyss; also in 9:19, the heads and tails of the horses, after the sixth trumpet	
Isaiah 11:6,	Revelation 7:17a	There is light at the end of the tunnel for every Christian. In the Sermon on the Mount (Matt. 5:5), Jesus predicted, "Blessed are the meek for they shall inherit the earth" (NASB). There is calm after the storm. An eternal peace awaits God's people.
The Messianic kingdom: And the wolf will dwell with the lamb. (NASB)	"And God will wipe away every tear from their eyes" (NASB). Also in Revelation 11:15–18, at the seventh trumpet, Christ begins to reign. Angels sing a hallelujah chorus thanking Him.	
	Revelation 19	
	The victory/ wedding celebration.	
	Revelation 21	
	The New Jerusalem; 21:4: "and he will wipe away every tear from their eyes." (NASB)	

Isaiah	Revelation	Application
Isaiah 42:13–16	Revelation 19:11–16b	Romans 8:31
The Lord will march out like a mighty man.	And behold, a white horse, and he who sat on it is called faithful and true. (NASB)	"If God be for us, who can be against us?"
Isaiah 52:8–9	Revelation 21	Christ's second coming will be a joyous occasion for those who love him.
Christ's return to Zion.	The new heaven and the new earth	
Isaiah 54:11–12	Revelation 21:10, 18–21	The place of many mansions God is preparing for us would be too dazzling for sinful earthly eyes.
The new city on a foundation of jewels	"He showed me the great city, the holy Jerusalem."	
Isaiah 62:11b	Revelation 22:7, 12	Jesus is bringing us a reward for our faithfulness to Him.
"Lo, your salvation comes; Behold His reward is with Him." (NASB)	Jesus is coming; he promises blessings to the faithful.	
Isaiah 65:17	Revelation 21:4b	Out with the old, in with the new. For God's people, joy replaces sadness.
"For behold, I create new heavens and a new earth." (NASB)	"For the former things have passed away." (NKJV)	

Study Questions

Choose the correct answer.

1. What king had just died when Isaiah got his call from the Lord to prophesy? (Jeroboam/Uzziah) _____

   _____

   _____

2. In What chapter do we hear about Isaiah's calling? (Chapter 1/Chapter 6) _____

   _____

3. What was the name of Isaiah's father? (Amoz/Amittai)

   _____

4. What does the name *Isaiah* mean? ("He grasps the heal" /"The Lord saves") _____

   _____-

5. Name three prophets who were contemporaries of Isaiah. Choose three. (Ezekiel/Jeremiah/Daniel or Amos/Hosea/ Micah) _____, _____,

   and _____.

The Relevance of Isaiah
in the Life of Contemporary Christianity

Isaiah got his calling at an interesting time. He speaks about it in chapter 6. Uzziah, the king and relative of Isaiah who had been one of the best kings of all time, tempted God through pride at the end of his reign and died a shamed (and punished—with leprosy!) man. God brought Judah's great king down low, and then he died. Isaiah, a short time later, had a vision of God exalted and raised up on his throne. The contrast is striking. God still today brings low those who oppose Him. He exalts those who acknowledge and honor him. Our nation and its leaders have been lowered—both in the eyes of our own people and in the eyes of the world. God does not take kindly to mocking. There are many who want to mock or ignore the Lord. We pray the Lord will lift up strong Christian leaders and pastors to reflect the glory of Christ. The Lord opposes the proud but draws near to the humble (James says in chapter 4:6, rephrasing an idea found in Isaiah 54:7, by the way). "Learn to do good. Seek justice. Reprove the ruthless. Defend the orphan. Plead for the widow," Isaiah says in chapter 1:17 (NASB). No matter how far we have strayed, however, God's mercy stands out as a lighthouse beacon of hope in the midst of a storm: "'Come now, and let us reason together,' says the Lord: 'Though your sins are as scarlet, they will be as white as snow'" (Isa. 1:18a, NASB).

We do not have to sit idly by and watch our elected officials rewrite laws favoring sins that God condemns in the Bible. Laws that favor same-sex marriage are an example. *Roe v. Wade* (1973) that legalized abortion is another. We can resist whatever other changes, finally, that defy what all Bible-loving, Christ-following people know to be right. We can do this by exercising our Christian liberty and First Amendment freedom of speech. We need to hold our pastors accountable, furthermore, for preaching strong messages of righteousness and a return to God's commands and will for our lives. May we never tire of standing up for Jesus and the sacred truths of Scripture, exemplified by the words of Isaiah, Shakespeare of the Old Testament.

Isaiah

In the year of King Uzziah's death
The Lord called on Isaiah.
The vision took away his breath:
God enthroned with seraphim!

"I am a man of unclean lips.
Now surely I must die."[10]
With coal of fire touching lips,
The seraph said, "Forgiven."

Sixty-six chapters are in this book.
Sixty-six books the Bible holds.
Our Lord, his words more often took
As quotes, then newly told.

No other prophet
Was quoted so much
By Jesus and yet
Of the Lord's powers, he had only a touch.

"Though your sins are as scarlet
They are white as snow.
Though they are red like crimson
They'll be as wool."[11]

"Wolf will lie down with lamb,"
Says chapter eleven and six.
Pets of the great "I am?"
It is an end-times millennium fix.

Isaiah gets a *Valley of Vision*,[12]
A God-sent "cinema."
For the showing of horror
Scenes, attractions yet to come.

Chapter thirty-two: a glorious future[13]
Where dysfunction is a thing of the past,
Where all faculties of his people are sure
Where righteousness and peace will last.[14]

In chapters fifty-three and four
We see the Suffering Servant:
Despised, rejected, Man of Sorrows
Tormented, tortured, slaughtered.

No one like son of Amoz
So clearly saw the passion.
Few like "The Lord saves"
Was blessed with such clarity of vision.

"The spirit of God is upon me."
Sixty-one, verse one and two.
Jesus then said it was He—
The Son of God foretold.[15]

"How beautiful are the feet
Of those who bring good news."[16]
This prophet could but repeat
God's message to all who would choose

To listen. If Isaiah lost his life
To wicked King Manasseh.
This loss was heaven's gain—
He is serving now his Master.

Notes

1. Uzziah, a relative of Isaiah, was a good king who finished badly, desecrating God's temple and usurping the role of the priests for which God punished him with leprosy for the rest of his life. Someone should say something to America's judges for usurping the role of the legislature in our day and age!

2. In Jeremiah 15:4, the prophet singles out Manasseh for ignominy. In taking the prophet's life, the evil king sets a precedent for the likes of Herod in Jesus's day, who killed John the Baptist for preaching against Herod's wickedness.

3. *Unger's Bible Handbook* (Chicago: Moody Press, 1966), 306–7 passim.

4. ESV, 585

5. Ancient pagan Greeks of the Classical Age (500–400 BC) warned of hubris—any mortal who dared, in their arrogance, to vie for the power of the gods. Too bad they did not know about the one true God of the Hebrews, active, with a long history of involvement, at the eastern end of the Mediterranean.

6. The Lenten hymn "Stricken, Smitten, and Afflicted": text by Thomas Kelly, 1769–1855, tune from *Geistliche Volkslieder*, by Paderborn, 1850 is an example. In addition, some estimates say that there are at least three hun-

dred Messianic prophecies from the Old Testament that Jesus fulfilled. Some are more detailed than others are. Those from Isaiah 53 are examples of detailed predictions. Someone has said that in view of the three hundred prophecies mentioned, the odds of Jesus not being the one described are like finding one exact quarter from a pile ten feet deep, covering the entire state of Texas— one in that many quarters, one over that many zeroes!

7. NASB, page 1032 notes how the Lord used Assyria and Babylonia to chastise His people. He is an author of evil for those who disobey—believer or unbeliever. R. C. Sproul, in his book *Knowing Scripture*, ([Downers Grove, Illinois: Intervarsity Press, 1967], 86–87) outlines how God sometimes intends evil against those who do evil against him and his commandments.

8. There may be a flip side to this blessing, which, if true, would turn this into one of those "be careful what you wish for" or, as the ancient Romans used to say, "caveat emptor" (let the buyer beware). During these extra years of life granted to Hezekiah, a son was born by the name of Manasseh. Manasseh turned out to be perhaps the most wicked king ever. He was Ahab revisited, if you will. Tradition says Manasseh was responsible for the horrible death of Isaiah (saying he put the prophet into the hollow of a tree stump and sawed him in half while still alive).

9. NASB, page 1014 says, "The Servant will mend broken lives."
10. Isaiah 6:5—contained in the call and commission of Isaiah, chapter 6 of Isaiah
11. Isaiah 1:18
12. Ibid. Chapter 22 describes the military punishments, which will befall his people in this valley.
13. Isaiah 32:1 begins to give a glimpse of the Messianic Age (NASB, 1000)
14. Ibid. verses 17–18
15. Luke 4:21, spoken just after quoting Isaiah 61:1 ff., during a Sabbath temple service. When he went on to elaborate that since the Hebrews of old had rejected God's will for their lives, the Gentiles were going to receive God's blessing for the future. At that point, the people, in rage, began to run the Son of God out of town.
16. Ibid., 52

[note to layout: insert photo 4; centralize]

Baruch, faithful secretary to Jeremiah, wrote down the words as God delivered them to the weeping prophet.

Jeremiah

בטרם   ידעתיך בטן אצרך ב אצורך

Before I formed you in the womb, I knew you
[going on to say, "And before you were born,
I consecrated you; I have appointed you a prophet
to the nations].

—Jeremiah 1:5a (NASB)

HIS NAME MEANS either "the Lord exalts" or "the Lord establishes," or possibly "the Lord throws" or "hurls." Since there are several passages in the prophet that use the verb "to hurl," we can assume a pun would have been intended, related to the meaning of his name, "He hurls." Jeremiah comes from the Babylonian period. He had been born in Anatoth, north of Jerusalem, in the territory of Benjamin. Called to the ministry in about 627 BC, God spoke through him during the last five kings of Judah leading up to the Babylonian invasion and captivity. He prophesied during the southern kingdom's decline and fall, therefore.[1]

As with the fall of the northern ten tribes to the Assyrians a century earlier, Babylon's invasion of Judah occurred in phases: first in 605 BC, followed by a second in 586 BC.

As for the prophet himself, who experienced these dark days for Jerusalem, Judah, and God's remaining chosen people—when given a choice by the invaders to stay, go to Babylon, or go to Egypt (discussed in Jeremiah 40:2–6)—Jeremiah was forced to flee with some (including Baruch, his secretary) to Egypt.[2]

Tradition says he was eventually stoned to death in the land of the Pharaohs. He resembles Isaiah in a couple of interesting ways; his ministry began under a good king, Josiah.[3]

Secondly, he witnessed the defeat and deportation of his people. In addition, both prophets were despised by many of their own people, Isaiah rumored to have been tortured and killed by wicked Manasseh, Jeremiah coming close to death a number of times, then finally, again according to tradition, dying in Egypt by stoning.[4]

Zephaniah served just prior to Jeremiah. Contemporaries would have included Habakkuk and, some say (but not this author), Obadiah. There are sections in Jeremiah that carry the trademark Habakkuk dialogue between God and His prophet. In like manner, there are passages in Jeremiah that carry references to Judah behaving like a prostitute, which remind us of Hosea. Isaiah also contains both elements. Both Isaiah and Jeremiah, furthermore, contain parts, which correspond with sections from the historical books of 1 and 2 Kings.

In this way, they show their awareness of others of God's representatives as well as being trailblazers, through God's anointing upon them, of something new and unique.

Following a long tradition (among Hebrew prophets and leaders) of drawing back in humility at God's initial calling to serve, Jeremiah's excuse was "I'm too young."[5]

By deduction, scholars have been able to ascertain that Jeremiah may have been a teenager when God called him to service under good King Josiah (Josiah, again, being grandson of wicked Manasseh).[6]

Every time that Jeremiah weeps for the people, seeing and knowing the punishment that is to come upon them for their rebellion and apostasy, he shares in a grief similar to the sadness our Lord felt knowing that many were rejecting Him and would continue to reject Him. Recall Jesus's words leading up to His passion: "Oh Jerusalem, Jerusalem, how often I have longed to gather your children as a hen gathers her chicks but you would not" (Matt. 23:37) comes to mind.

Jeremiah's steadfastness in the face of suffering and persecution recall the passion of Christ who continued to reach out to the world, even as he lost his own freedom, comfort, and absence of pain. Jesus never ceased asking God to forgive his enemies, offering eternal life to those who would humble themselves and accept him as Lord and Savior. Jeremiah never tired of delivering God's truth, his message of punishment for those who chose sin and rebellion, his message of peace and forgiveness for those who would seek a relationship with God who always waits, in mercy, to pardon the penitent.

Themes in Jeremiah[7]

Well-Known Passages

Challenge yourself to see how many of these passages you remember. Try to learn more of them and learn them better than you know them already. Some of the words here are paraphrases; others are more word for word.

> 1:5: "Before I formed you in the womb, I knew you and before you were born I consecrated you; I have appointed you a prophet to the nations" (NASB) [the first part is a strong Biblical proof passage that argues for the sanctity of life in the mother's womb].

2:16b: whereby they have forsaken Me and have offered sacrifices to other gods, one of the main reasons for God's displeasure with His chosen covenanted people—a violation of the First Commandment: thou shalt have no other gods; our "idols" today are anything or person that regularly takes up great amounts of our time and devotion].

2:13b: They have forsaken Me, The fountain of living waters, To hew for themselves cisterns, Broken cisterns That can hold no water. [Jesus said to the woman of Samaria at the well that she could drink of the "living water", that was Jesus (John 4:13). Jesus claimed full divinity when he said, "I and the Father are one." Therefore, Jehovah's Witnesses and others are wrong when they say the Father created, and therefore is superior to, the Son. Such groups are drawing from broken cisterns].

5:1: "Run to and fro through the streets of Jerusalem and seek...if you can find a man...who executes judgment, and I will pardon her" (NASB) [sounds like Sodom and Gomorrah—even there God would have spared the cities if only ten righteous persons were found (Gen. 18:32). Those were pagan cities. These were God's people and it seems there was not even one, except for Jeremiah and Baruch, his assistant. Consider also Elijah's complaint to the Lord during the cave experience when Elijah was down and out after the slaying of the prophets of Baal and Asherah leading to Elijah's subsequent flight from wicked Queen Jezebel. There the prophet had complained he was the only one left proclaiming the truth. God told the one he loved that at this time, there were yet "Seven thousand who have not yet bowed the knee to Baal"].

5:8: They [the men of Israel] were well-fed, lusty stallions; every one neighed after his neighbor's wife (NASB) [Why do we continually have the Hollywood culture thrust in front of our faces—those whose lifestyles fly in the face of God's blessing upon the "one man for one woman for a lifetime" concept? Know of any "swingers" in your circle of friends? Stop associating with them and warn them of how they are headed down the wide pathway of the pagan, the one that leads to eternal death and separation from God.]

8:22: Is there no balm in Gilead [Judah, the southern kingdom], is there no physician there? (NASB) [no one who cares to keep the people righteous before a righteous God]?[8]

12:1b: Why has the way of the wicked prospered? Why are all those who deal in treachery at ease? (NASB) Which one of us has not had similar feelings? On the flip side, why do bad things happen to good people—God's people? Answer: It is our predicament due to the sin we have inherited from Adam and Eve.]

23:5: "Behold, the days are coming," declares the LORD, "When I will raise up for David a righteous Branch; And He will reign as king and act wisely And do justice and righteousness in the land" (NASB). [This is a Messianic prophecy.]

29:11: "For I know the plans I have for you," declares the Lord, "plans for welfare and not for calamity to give you a future and a hope" (NASB) [It is a classic and beautiful passage, full of love and comfort for God's children].

31:15a: Thus says the Lord: "A voice ws heard in Ramah, lamentation and bitter weeping, Rachel

weeping f or her children" (NASB) [quoted in
Matthew 2:18—fulfilled during Herod's murder
of the male babies two years old and under, after
Herod found out from the unsuspecting wise men
that Jesus, a king, had been born in Bethlehem.
Herod only saw Him as a rival to his throne. He did
not realize it was a spiritual kingdom Christ would
rule and point others to, coming in peace, not to
make war or steal earthly thrones].

Specific Sins

Once again, of how many of these offenses against God
would we and our leaders, both within the church and
without, be judged guilty today by a righteous God? Let
us pledge to identify, admit, confess, seek forgiveness for
(through prayer) and make right with the Lord the wrongs
we have committed.

> 6:5–6: Unjust dealings, oppression of their own
> people.

> 7:5–9: Shedding innocent blood, following other
> gods, stealing, murder, committing adultery, pur-
> gery, burning incense to Baal.

7:31: Building high places [for worshiping false gods] in the Valley of Ben Hinnom [where they burned and sacrificed their own sons and daughters].

8:2: Worshiping the sun, moon, and stars; consulting the same. [Astrology: Some people follow this today, in the name of something cool to do, as in: What sign were you born under? It is a bad choice, by God's standards.]

8:6: No one repents. [Does our mass media sometimes champion the rebel and outlaw? How will that bit of mischievous fun lead us to a more repentant heart as a nation?]

8:10: All are greedy for gain [the almighty dollar: history has repeated itself throughout the ages]; prophets and priests alike, all practice deceit.

8:12: They have no shame.

9:3: They are liars [the last three passages all show what happens when money blinds you, becoming an idol in your life. You become like a drug addict who will do anything: beg, borrow, or steal to get what you want—your addiction].

9:13: They have forsaken the law.

9:14: They have followed the Baals.

11:10: They have broken the Mosaic Covenant.

11:13: As many gods as cities [a bar on every corner in many towns in America today, the sex industry, materialism, humanism or the glorification of man, and more].

29:23: because they [the false prophets] have acted foolishly in Israel, and have committed adultery with their neighbors' wives and have spoken words in my name falsely [some of our biggest name Christian ministers have fallen into adultery with prostitutes].

44:16 ff.: "As for the word that you have spoken to us, in the name of the lord, we will not listen to you!" (NKJV) [words of defiance from the people to Jeremiah. Several popular secular songs put sex, drugs, and rock and roll on a pedestal].

Metaphors and Similes for Wickedness

3:22: [God's people are] backsliders.

4:3: [They are] sowing among thorns

4:4: [God's people have] foreskins around the heart.

6:7: She pours out her wickedness like a well pouring out water.

6:30: [They have become] rejected silver [God tried to refine them, but they refused].

They Think They're Innocent: None So Blind As Those Who Will Not See

2:35a: Yet you said "I am innocent." (NASB)

3:23: Idolatrous dealings in the high places are a deception.

5:12–13: They said, "They have lied about the Lord and said, 'Not he; Misfortune will not come on us, and we will not see sword or famine.'" (NASB) [Nebuchadnezzar's siege of Jerusalem women were cooking their own dead infants to keep from starving].

6:14: [Prophets and priests] dress the wound of my people as though it were not serious.

8:8a: How can you say, "We are wise?" (NASB)

Judah Is in Shame

3:24–25: Let us lie down in our shame. (NASB) [What has happened to shame in our culture? God suggests even a little shame helps us hold one another up to an accounting for our actions and words].

6:15: They were not even ashamed at all (NASB) [and someone needs to hold us up to shame whenever we act shamefully. Shame is kind of like a public display of what a healthy active conscience should have told us all along was wrong].

9:2b: For they are all adulterers [reminds of James 4:4, "You adulteresses, do you not know that friendship with the world is hostility toward God?"]. (NASB)

How great is our shame!

God's Punishment

As in Isaiah, Micah, and other prophets, the opening message is one of judgment and punishment for God's people.

5:14b: Behold, I am making My words in your mouth fire And this people wood, and it will consume them. (NASB)

8:17: Vipers coming [Babylon].

9:11: I will make Jerusalem a heap of ruins. (NASB) [Jesus predicted this also; it occurred forty years after His ascension.]

9:15: "Behold, I will feed them, this people, with wormwood and give them poisoned water to drink." (NASB)

9:16a: I will scatter them among the nations. (NASB) [The diaspora occurred in 70 AD and was not undone until spring of 1948, when the world and the Lord finally reinstated the nation of Israel.]

9:22b: The dead bodies of men will fall like dung on the open field. (NASB)

29:17: "Behold, I am sending upon them the sword, famine and pestilence." (NASB)

29:24: Punishment for Shemaiah, the false prophet [eventually killed for leading astray God's people. "Beware of false prophets who come to you in sheep's clothing, but inwardly they are ravening wolves"—Jesus from the Sermon on the Mount (Matt. 7:15)].

Metaphors and Similes for Punishment

23:19: The storm of the Lord, a whirlwind swirling down on the heads of the wicked.

25:15: Cause the nations to drink the cup of God's wrath.

25:24: I am calling down a sword upon all who live on the earth.

25:27b: Fall and rise no more because of the sword I will send among you. (NASB)

25:30b: He will shout like those who tread the grapes. (NASB)

27:12: Bring your necks under the yoke of the king of Babylon (NSAB) [picture Nebuchadnezzar at the plow and the wicked sons of Judah yoked, their just dessert, to the plow, doing their new king's bidding].

30:23: Behold, the tempest of the LORD! Wrath has gone forth (NASB) [reminds me of the last booming thunder and lightning storm I experienced].

47:2: The waters will become an overflowing torrent [Jesus, the water of life for the Samaritan woman and for all sinners, can and will show His other side when Nebuchadnezzar does His bidding, punishing Jerusalem. He will do it one final time for all at the end of times].

49:33: Hazor will become a haunt of jackals (NASB) [when man loses his God-appointed sovereignty over the beasts, it shows that God, like the people abandoning the territory in question, has left His people. Without God's protection (the One who holds all things together as described in Colossians) wild animals take over—not a pretty picture. Like an unrated bad movie, life without God is barren, hopeless, and terrifying. You do not want to go there or be a part of this. Stand up for righteousness and do not let this happen to your family, your community, your state, your nation, our world!].

49:37: I will scatter them [Elam] to the four winds.

Metaphors and Similes for Enemies of Judah

3:7: A lion [Babylon] has gone up from his thicket.

4:4: A scorching wind, blowing from the desert is coming [Babylon].

4:13: Behold he [Babylon] goes up like clouds. (NASB)

5:6: A lion from the forest, a wolf from the desert, a leopard lying in wait [the same three animals that will be tamed, as mentioned in Isaiah 11:6 ff., at the end of times].

6:23: Their voice roars like the sea [not the pleasant roaring, a soothing sound, on a nice day, but more like the blustery sound on a stormy one].

Metaphors for Repentance

4:8: For this, put on sackcloth, lament, and wail. (NASB)

A Remnant

Although the majority of the prophetic messages were warnings of coming punishment, often thematic was the promise of a remnant. We can see this doctrine as a kind of anti-theme against the godless theory of evolution, which says only the strong survive (presently leading so many young people astray in our public schools). In this case, the strong in faith, the penitent, and the seekers after the heart of the Lord will survive and will meet up with all believers in heaven one day.

> 5:18: Yet, even in those days declares the LORD, "I will not make you a complete destruction." (NASB)

> 23:3: Then I myself will gather the remnant. (NASB)

> Chapter 30, all and specifically

> 30:7: He (Jacob) will be saved. (NASB)

> 30:17: "For I will restore you to health." (NASB)

> 31:37: Thus says the LORD, "If the heavens above can be measured And the foundations of the earth

searched out below, Then I will also cast off all the offspring of Israel." [what logicians call a future, contrary to fact, condition].

33:15: In those days and at that time I will cause a righteous branch of David to spring forth. (NASB)

40:11: Jews from surrounding territories heard that the king of Babylon had left a remnant behind and they came back to settle there.

44:7: God asks people turning from Him to go to Egypt against His will not to jeopardize their future as a surviving remnant; He even threatens there will be no remnant.

46:27–28: God will surely save Israel.

Unabashed Praise for a Wonderful God

Even the great weeping prophet, who hardly saw a soul turned by God's message through him in forty years of ministry, had to pause once in a while and offer a positive message of praise and adoration for his mighty, loving, jealous, and just God:

10:6–10: No one is like you, oh Lord; you are great. [Do you perceive the influence of the Psalms here?] (NASB)

Passages Harking Back to Creation

4:23–26: [The passage depicts an anti-creation scene, to symbolize destruction coming]

4:28: I beheld the earth and, lo, it was without form and void [וּבֹהוּ ו ווה (*tohu va vohu*) as in Genesis 1:2).

Rhetorical Questions in Jeremiah

The great prophets, the major prophets, and even some of the minor prophets resort to many different literary devices to get their point across, as God, the Holy Spirit, speaks through them. One method is the rhetorical question (often spoken and interpreted in a tone of sarcasm). Try some of these on for size and see if God would have cause to speak to his children this way in our day and age:

2:32: Can a maid forget her ornaments [I am thinking of my wife. Are you?], or a bride, her attire? (KJV)

8:4: Do men fall and not get up again? Does one turn away and not repent? (NASB) [unless you want to roll around on the ground like a worm, or unless you are in need of Life Alert.]

18:14: Does the snow of Lebanon [or Wisconsin, or Buffalo, New York, or Montana during the winter] forsake the rock of the open country? (NASB)

23:23: Am I only a god nearby? (NIV)

23:24a: Can anyone hide himself in hiding places so I don't see him? (NASB) [invoking a picture of the post-fall Adam and Eve in the garden.]

23:24b: "Do I not fill the heavens and the earth?" declares the Lord. (NASB) [in a majestic expression of sovereignty].

23:29: [Another in a series from chapter 23] Is not my word like fire…and like a hammer? (NASB)

30:6 Ask now, and see If a male can give birth. [except in his dreams or when playacting]?

31:20: Is Ephraim [Judah] my dear son? (NASB) [Expecting a "yes" answer: God asks in a moment of affection for a faithful people presently gone astray.]

49:19: For who is like me, and who will summon me into court? And who then is the shepherd who can stand against me? (NASB). The truth brought even mighty King David, who graduated from shepherd boy to invincible warrior, to his knees in sackcloth and ashes at the death of his firstborn with Bathsheba. He had to accept his punishment from God for a sinner's adultery and murder.

Comparison: Jeremiah, Revelation, and a Personal Application

Jeremiah	Revelation	Application
They…have offered sacrifices to other gods (1:16, NASB)	The rest of mankind…did not repent…so as not to give up worshiping demons (9:20, NASB)	People who honor the devil end up in the burning lake of fire prepared for Satan and followers.
Israel was holy to the Lord, the first of His Harvest (Jer. 2:3, NASB)	These are the ones who follow the Lamb. They have been purchased from among men (the 144,000 in heavenly Jerusalem).	All believers in Christ share in God's kingdom: "But you are a chosen race, a royal priesthood" (1 Pet. 2:9a, NASB).
"Do you not fear Me?" declares the Lord (Jer. 5:22, (NASB).	"Who will not fear, O Lord, And glorify Your name?" [sung by end-time martyrs, inspired by the Song of Moses] (Rev. 15:4a, NASB)	Those who fear the Lord and glorify His name in this world will be blessed. [The Lord] Who crowns you with lovingkindness and compassion (Ps. 103:4 b, NASB).

Study Questions

Choose one.

1. What does the name *Jeremiah* mean? ("The Lord exalts"/ "Called by God") _____
2. What was the name of Jeremiah's birthplace? (Bethlehem/Anatoth) _____
3. In what tribal territory was Jeremiah's hometown located? (Judah/Benjamin) _____
4. Name two kings Jeremiah served under. (Uzziah and Ahab/Josiah and Jehoiakim) _____ _____ and _____
5. What was going on in Judah's history toward the end of his service as prophet? (Assyria was destroying the northern kingdom/ The Babylonians were overrunning the southern kingdom) _____

_____

What Jeremiah Means to Us Today

When Jeremiah spoke of Israel in Jeremiah 2:3, to whom was he referring? Dr. Hocking believes he has captured the Scriptural completeness of that term:

1) From Genesis 32:28, it is the new name for Jacob (after his wrestling match with an angel). In so doing, (my extension) he went from (JAACOV) "He grasps the heal" or "Jacob" to (YISRAEL) "He wrestles with God."

2) The physical descendants of Abraham, Isaac, and Jacob

3) The nation (from Deuteronomy 31:7–8)

4) The land promised (Gen. 17:8, 26:3; Ps. 105:8–11)

5) Jews who became believers (Gal. 6:16)

6) God Himself, 108 times—"Lord God of Israel," 203 times "God of Israel." In other words, when "Israel" is mentioned, it sometimes can even refer to the God of Israel, the Yahweh we all know and love—our Divine King Himself (according to Dr. Hocking)!

7) The "dry bones" that will live again (Ezek. 37:11–14).[9]

In addition, the mention of "Jacob's Trouble" in Jeremiah 30:5–7 coupled with "The Day of the Lord" is a key component of the tribulation at the end of times. Several passages from our Old Testament prophets (as well as Jesus's key discussion in Matthew 24 and in Revelation itself) speak of this time: Joel 2:11, Zephaniah 1:14, Joel 1:15, Daniel 12:1, Joel 2:2, and Matthew 24:21 and Revelation 16:18.[10]

Jeremiah

A teen from Anatoth,
The tribe of Benjamin,
Was chosen both
To promote good and dissuade from sin.

"Before I formed you in the womb,
Before, then, you were born
I knew and consecrated you.
Israel: Be warned!

"Don't fear their faces."[11]
"I'm but a youth; can I share truth
With people of all ages?"[12]
With coals, the angel touched his mouth:

"You shall pluck up and even break down,
Destroy and overthrow.
Your words shall build and plant.
The world no doubt will know.

Your commission is from God."[13]
Josiah good, Jehoiakim bad—
Two kings our prophet served.[14]
"The Lord Exalts" was glad

To do his Sovereign's bidding:
"Backsliders, thorns, uncircumcised,"
He chided with words quite fitting.
Their sins he emphasized.

The "Weeping Prophet" cried,
A plea for righteousness.
Even Baruch, no doubt, tried
To straighten out the mess.

In chains, the enemy found him
When Babylon burst through the gates.[15]
Still true to his calling,
Trusting God, not fates.

They say he died in pharaoh land,
Baruch in his employ.
God's witness to the end,
His tears now turned to joy.

Notes

1. Nelson, page 309
2. Jeremiah 42:14–16 and 18–19, 21–22 and elsewhere show Jeremiah warning the people that God's hand of judgment will fall severely upon their heads if they go to Egypt. We, therefore, know that the prophet would never have gone to Egypt willingly. Then he shows up in 43:6 along with Baruch. Others had forced him to go. Tradition, if true, bears out that he and Baruch themselves fell under the same deadly curse that God had warned Johanan and the other military leaders about, through Jeremiah.
3. Isaiah began under Uzziah, a relative, who fell from God's good graces toward the end of his reign and received the punishment of leprosy for presuming to assume some of the tasks of the priests.
4. Jeremiah 42 is all about God's warning to His people not to flee into Egypt. Jeremiah 42:16, in fact, says they will die by the sword there. The prophet clearly sees by the end of this chapter, however, that the people are bent on going to Egypt anyway. There is irony in the fact that the prophet, if tradition is true, died in the very place and in the same way God prophesied in warning to His people in 42:16. Jeremiah 43:6–7 reveal a rebellious few people, Jeremiah and Baruch in tow,

making their way to Egypt and their doom, a judgment from God.

5. Jeremiah 1:6

6. How many a young pastor has thought or uttered similar misgivings? Yours truly was a seminarian for nearly two years (in the mid eighties). As my time to go out under the wings of a senior pastor approached, I too wondered how I would win over the elders of the congregation. *How would they ever respect a young upstart like me?* I mused. With God's help, I would have gotten my response.

7. As you look at the themes, read the beginnings of the passages chosen under each theme heading. The intended effect is that you will begin to form a picture of Jeremiah—his giftedness, the variety of subject matter, how he fits in with the time in which he served and lived. When the picture becomes more rich and varied, let the experience become like thumbing through a picture album. Some will know the rest of these passages. Many will be able to fill in the blanks. Others will just be learning. Whatever your level of familiarity with this prophet and his writings, look up the rest of the passage when the Spirit moves you. This aid intends to get you into God's Word after all. God bless your reading, imagining, filling in the blanks, album thumbing, and Bible study.

8. NASB, page 1069, notes how Gilead enjoyed its blessing literally "as an important source of spices and medicinal herbs."

9. Moses offered at least four objections, one being that he was not eloquent of speech (Exod. 3–4); Gideon, in Judges 6:15, protested that his family, tribe of Manasseh, was least in the tribe and he was youngest in his family.

10. NASB, footnote on Jeremiah 30:7, p.1104, mentions how the reference in Jeremiah applies both to "the immediate future," perhaps described in Jeremiah 8:18, as well as to "a more remote time in the Messianic Age."

11. Jeremiah 1:5

12. Ibid., 1:6

13. Ibid., 1:10

14. "Two kings" among others, that is. Others included Jehoahaz, Jehoiakin, and Zedekiah.

15. Jeremiah 39:14 says the Babylonian conquerors found and released Jeremiah from the guardhouse where they had kept him during the last days prior to Jerusalem's capture.

[note to layout: insert photo; centralize]

The people mourn the destruction and death at the fall of Jerusalem, to Babylon. May we not let our faith lag, dooming us to destruction.

Lamentations

בגוים   איבה   רבתי כאלמנה היתה עם רבתי העיר בדד ישבה

How lonely sits the city that was full of
people! She has become like a widow.

—Lamentations 1:1a (NASB)

THE HEBREW TITLE of the book is *Ekah* ("How!"), also
the first word of the work. Although there is no claim of
authorship within Lamentations itself, both the Greek
Septuagint and the Latin Vulgate translations attributed it
to Jeremiah, the weeping prophet.[1]

I have included this book here mostly because English
Bibles have placed it among the prophets, after Jeremiah—
the supposed author. The Hebrew Bible, instead, included it
in the third section—the Ketuvim (or writings) as opposed
to the Nevi'im (or prophets).[2]

The short book consists of a series of five poems. The author allots each poem its own chapter. In the first poem, the predominant technique involves the anguished third person musings of an omniscient author. The author is omniscient but not in the theological sense reserved for God. He is omniscient only in seeing and reporting what his eyes have seen. He sees all. Hindsight may be twenty-twenty. When used in the service of God's spokesperson, it promises a one hundred percent dividend in relaying the pitiable state to which unrighteousness and wickedness will reduce us. In Lamentations 1:16, the prophet shares how the waterworks in his eyes have been turned to the full. He explains, "Because far from me is a comforter."

The Holy Spirit is a Comforter. The Holy Spirit, part of the divine and holy trinity, cannot reside where there is rampant and wanton desertion of God's laws. Here is a poignant demonstration of what hell will be like, the worst part of which will be an eternal banishment from God's comforting presence.

The derision of enemies (described in Lamentations 2:16–17 as well as Lamentations. 3:46) expresses how salt rubbed into the wounds increased the agony of a people who once enjoyed enviable prosperity and protection from a loving and protecting God.

Psalm 137:7 (NASB) sung from the bowels of captivity in Babylon and captured the specific words of the Edomites.

The latter, in the midst of burning, pillage, destruction, and rape, yelled, "Raze it; raze it [Jerusalem] to its very foundation."

When the author begins walking down the streets of the devastated Jerusalem, he sees the "bride" that Jesus would later speak of as having lost everything. She had made her bed. Now she would sleep in it. Lamentations 1:9 (NASB) says, "Her uncleanness was in her skirts."

God demanded a virgin bride. Jerusalem and Judah had opened itself up to any and all takers. By the time of Christ, Herod the Great had rebuilt a beautiful new temple and was restoring Jerusalem. Yet, once again, the people made themselves ripe for destruction. The blinded spiritual eyes of the hypocritical Pharisees and the unbelieving Sadducees would not allow many to see the Messiah when he dwelt among them, almost daily fulfilling prophecies before their very eyes. John, the disciple Jesus loved, describes this well in John 1:11 (NASB), where he says, "He came to his own, and those who were his own did not receive him."

To the women who wept for Jesus on the Via Dolorosa, the Lord responded, "Weep for yourselves" (described in Luke 23:28–31). To His disciples, concerning the temple, He foretold, "Not one stone] here will be left on another" (Matt. 24:2, NASB). The destruction of the temple and diaspora of the people brought this to fulfillment in 70 AD. The seemingly hopeless state of affairs in Jerusalem as described in Lamentations would be a precursor for the Romans' destruction some 670 years later. Both events should put the fear of God in the heart of agnostics or weak believers. We create our own demise by submitting to sin rather than to our Savior.

Well- Known Passages

> 3:22–23, NASB: The Lord's loving kindnesses indeed never cease, for his compassions never fail, they are new every morning. Great is your faithfulness [lyrics to a well-known hymn].[3]

> 3:40, NASB: Let us examine and probe our ways, and let us return to the Lord.

Similes Abounding

The poet, a builder of pictures through words, receives from the Lord what elementary school teachers of Spanish like to refer to as *palabras poderosas*, "powerful words." The simile seems best able to accomplish his purpose. The inspired author speaks to the subject within the text itself when he asks (2:13): "To what shall I liken you? What shall I compare with you?" Simile and metaphor are among the chief figures of speech used by poets of many times and places for comparison. The Hebrew prophets are no exception. The difference is the literary techniques of the latter are inspired by, and designed to lead people to, God.

Here are some examples: "[Judah's princes fleeing] like deer" (1:6); "as in a winepress [was Judah trampled]" (1:15); "like a flaming fire [has the Lord blazed against Jacob]" (2:3); "like an enemy [the Lord has swallowed Israel]" (2:5); "like a river [her tears run down]" (2:18) [where the city wall is also personified] ; "like water [she pours out her heart]" (2:19).

Prosaic/Journalistic Brutal Honesty

In stark contrast to poetic simile and metaphor is the technique of no minced words, in-your-face reporting not unlike that of a modern newspaper correspondent who is on the scene. Examples are Judah "weeps bitterly in the night" (1:2); "tears are on her cheeks" (1:2); "all her friends...have become her enemies" (1:2). "The Lord determined to lay in ruins the wall [of Jerusalem]" (2:8). "[Infants] cry... 'Where is bread and wine?'" (2:12). "The hands of compassionate women have boiled their own children; they became their food" (4:10) notes the writer who is living this nightmare unraveling before him. During the time of Elisha, Benhadad (king of the Arameans) and King Jehoram of Israel, a similar cannibalism is described as having taken place during Ben-hadad's siege of Jerusalem—a time when mothers argued over the promise of cannibalizing each other's sons (2 Kings 6:24–30).

Mistakes of the People

Often the prophets foresaw God's punishment from a distance, based upon the people's wicked behavior (Isaiah and Joel, for example). Jeremiah was one who foresaw close at hand, actually experiencing the destruction firsthand, being forced to view and walk through the devastation. The king placed him in chains, severely punishing him for advising the king and Judah to repent and to give in to Nebuchadnezzar during the latter's siege of Jerusalem. Here is a summary of some of the mistakes as the writer recalls using his short-term memory: "Jerusalem sinned grievously; therefore, she has become an unclean thing in God's eyes" (1:8, NASB); "Her uncleanness was in her skirts" (1:9, NASB); Jerusalem confesses: "The Lord is righteous; For I have rebelled against His command" (1:18, NASB). One thing God detests is when "Your prophets have seen for you false and deceptive visions. They have not exposed your iniquity...but have seen for you oracles that are false" (2:14). "This was for the sins of her prophets and the iniquities of her priests, who shed in the midst of her the blood of the righteous" (4:13).

In our day, those nations (including our own) that have allowed abortion to creep into the legally sanctioned sphere are doing the same. God will call us all to account for this on Judgment Day and possibly even before. When you are involved in gross sin, you often do not know the cause of your misfortune, your lack of blessings from God. God is calling us to account in the here and now, just as he did during the dangerous and disastrous times of Jeremiah.

Enemies Rejoice at Jerusalem's Demise

If you accept an earlier date for Obadiah (800s BC), then the rejoicing of Edom had been common knowledge for a couple of centuries. Obadiah, the Old Testament's shortest book, had predicted that Edom would be there to gloat. Psalm 137:7b, NASB also records how they taunted: "Raze it; raze it to its very foundation." At Lamentations 1:21b (NASB) the prophet mentions how enemies, in general, "are glad that you have done it" (speaking to Babylon). Continuing in Lamentations 1:21 on to 1:22, we see a familiar sentiment: "How blessed will be the one who repays you with the recompense with which you have repaid us" (Ps.137:8, NASB, says the prophet, speaking for fallen Jerusalem, in a request to the Lord, to return the favor to Edom and other enemies who would find joy in Judah's suffering). Psalm 137:9, NASB, once again, echoes that sentiment: How blessed will be the one who seizes and dashes your little ones Against the rock" [just as Babylon had done to Jerusalem].

Americans of the twenty-first century know well the sting of enemies who taunt at us during a time of suffering. We saw Palestinians dancing in the streets, for example, after the September 11, 2001 attack on the Twin Towers. Those from the land of the free and the home of the brave did not forget, searing it into their memory, some secretly, some not so secretly, wishing evil on the enemies to our nation. Christians pray for their enemies, asking how God might use them to lead others to Christ.

Comparisons Abound

In chapter 4, the prophet nostalgically looks back on a golden age, when Israel's heroes were to die for, when her foes literally did fall like mown grass. The stark contrast between the former days of faithfulness and the recent past ones of an almost total falling away from the Lord have resulted in what the prophet now describes: "How the gold has grown dim" (4:1, ESV); "Her princes were purer than snow, whiter than milk" (4:7, ESV); "Their bodies were ruddier than coral, the beauty of their form was like sapphire" (4:7b, ESV).

What a change has taken place. The "purer than snow" and "whiter than milk" has changed. Now...their appearance is blacker than soot, They are not recognized in the streets; Their skin is shriveled on their bones, It is withered, it has become like wood (4:8, NASB).

Christians today long for the days when our country looked to God first, included Him in the midst of our daily public lives—in schools, in the law courts, in our homes. Pray we return to our golden age.

Comparison: Lamentations, Revelation, and a Personal Application

Lamentations	Revelation	Application
The Lord has trodden as in a winepress the virgin daughter of Judah (1:15b, NASB)	The winepress [of God's wrath] was trodden outside the city (14:20, NASB)	God prefers a harvest of souls for the kingdom but will concede to Satan a harvest of those who reject him.
They [the elders of the daughters of Zion] have thrown dust on their heads (2:10b, NASB)	They threw dust on their heads and were crying out [speaking of merchants] (18:19, NASB)	Before our rejoicing at Jesus' victory, we will see the mourning of unbelievers.

Lamentations	Revelation	Application
In dark places he's made me dwell (3:6, NASB).	A third of the sun and a third of the moon and a third of the stars were struck, so that a third of them would be darkened (8:12, NASB).	The children of light prefer the light. In Heaven the Lamb's glory will lighten our steps.

Study Questions

1. What is the meaning of the Hebrew title of the book (*Ekah*)? ("When?"/"How?") _____
2. What two ancient translations attribute authorship to Jeremiah? Choose two. (King James/Greek Septuagint/Latin Vulgate/NIV) _____ and _____
3. What is a nickname for the alleged author? (the Weeping Prophet/the Meek Prophet) _____ _____
4. How many poems comprise this short book? (Ten/five) _____
5. What part of the Hebrew Bible included this book? (Ketuvim or writings/Nevi'im or prophets) _____ _____

Lamentations Applies Today More than Ever

We Christians mourn the loss of innocence for our culture. There was a time when the laws of the land reflected much more accurately the will of the Lord for His people. We have never been a theocracy as were God's people in the Old Testament. Yet our founding fathers for the most part believed God's Word and used it as their guide in planning, writing, then executing the Constitution of the United States. When a nation jettisons all the best that God has to offer, including basic guidelines and laws from the Ten Commandments, we will thenceforward be depriving ourselves of many blessings. Whether or not we will undergo discipline should also not be in doubt. After all, look at what happened to Judah and Jerusalem as described in Lamentations. If God is the "same yesterday, today and forever," we should expect God to respond to what is happening in our world.

In Haggai, we learn that God was thwarting the best-laid plans of the people. Much of what they were doing did not come to fruition. The people did not even know it was due to their neglect of the Lord. How many of the bad things happening to us are due and will continue to be due our failure to be faithful to God and His word? Let us pray for ourselves, for our nation, and for a return to the God who created us, who loves us, who sustains us, but who also will chasten us many times in an attempt to win back his bride. In the spirit of Lamentations, we mourn for better times.

Lamentations

She who was once a princess
Now weeps bitterly in the night.
I was there. I heard this—
Aftermath of the fight.

Judah has gone into exile.
Just desserts for wickedness.
Yet I remain all the while
In mourning, under duress.

It pains to see my countrymen,
Groaning priests, virgins undone,
No one to help her.
Enemies mock her ruin.

My eyes run with water.
For these things, I weep.
God has lost his daughter
Ekah? How can I sleep?

My heart—beating inside my breast!
She ignored His pleadings.
He gave her His best,
Wasted proceedings.

I see the elders silent
With dust on their heads,
As they utter laments
For all of the dead.

My eyes now fail for tears.
My spirit is troubled.
All our worst fears
Have happened, been doubled.

Little ones beg for grain and drink
As they faint in the streets.
Seeing their afflictions
I pause to think

How often I had warned them of this,
How their God was righteous
Yet ready to kiss
Repentant hearts.

Remember, oh Lord,
And see our reproach.
Let *hope* be your word
At our future approach.

The joy is gone.
Our dancing—no more.
Renew us! You have won.
You have cut us to the core!

Ekah, the Hebrew
For this book,
Meaning "How?"
The first word of the work.

The OT's anonymous author—
Like Hebrews from the new.
A piece of history this one offers.
Hebrews—a bridge between old and new.

No one claiming authorship,
Yet evidence seems clear.
The "Weeping Prophet"
Once again, appears to shed a tear.

The city of David—personified.
Jerusalem mourns for itself.
So many people have died.
Proud Nazirites swept off the shelf.[4]

"How lonely sits the city...
She's like a widow now",
An object of pity.
Oh, Jerusalem, "how?"

Ekah, the Hebrew once again.
How could it finish thus?
No more the sins of men
Would stain God's righteousness.

Notes

1. Unger, p.361; also, the opening salvo, down to the eleventh verse, "we're cut to the core," is from the viewpoint of the prophet, told in the first person for effect, allowing for a bit of poetic license to invite a deeper experience of the hopelessness felt by survivors.
2. Ibid.
3. Written by Thomas Chisholm to a friend (William Runyan, who later put the words to music) in 1923 while on a missions trip away from home.
4. Lamentations 4:7–8 describes the striking contrast between how some of the best men looked before and how they appear now.

[note to layout: insert photo; centralize]

*God shows the prophet Ezekiel a vision, the Valley of Dry Bones
(Ezek. 37; explanation in 37:11–14, a reference to Israel).*[1]

Ezekiel

וארא והנה רוח סערה באה מן־הצפון

As I looked, behold, a storm wind
was coming from the north.

—Ezekiel 1:4 (NASB)

EZEKIEL, WHOSE NAME means "God strengthens," was married and came from a Zadokite priestly family. The meaning of his name would have held special significance for his
contemporaries, who were in need of hope and encouragement, due to their plight of captivity.

His father was Buzi (1:3). Ezekiel's wife died during
the siege of Jerusalem, in 588 BC (24:1, 15–18). The Lord
referred to her as "the desire of your eyes" (24:16). Having
been told his wife would die the day Jerusalem fell (24:15–
22), such a day could not have been sadder for any man of

God. Not only would he allow the prophet's wife to die, God also commanded him not to grieve her death. To the eyes of most, the Lord appears to be a hard taskmaster at times. However, from God's perspective, difficult times call for difficult measures.[2]

Deported in 597 BC (the second deportation) with King Jehoiachin when he was about twenty-five years old, he lived his life ministering to God's people during the Babylonian captivity period.[3] It appears Ezekiel may have begun his prophetic ministry at the age of thirty, receiving his last vision around the age of fifty. According to Numbers 4, those were the exact years suggested for the active service of priests—which a function Ezekiel also performed.[4]

As such, perhaps God, through Ezekiel's ministry, is making a statement that this captivity was his ideal for all a prophet and priest could be or hope to be. He was willing to be in humble submission to his Lord.

Jeremiah had been prophesying since midway through the reign of Josiah (640–609 BC), and he would continue God's service into the reigns of four more kings. He was not among those deported but, instead, experienced the fall of Jerusalem in 586 BC, fleeing to Egypt with Baruch from which experience, we believe, he never returned. The Babylonians carried Ezekiel off into exile in 597 BC. He would have heard only later about Jerusalem's destruction from afar. Daniel, for his part, had been ministering to the

Lord in high places in Babylon since his participation in the first deportation of 605 BC. Perhaps he and Ezekiel knew one another.

When God told his prophet he was about to deprive him of the "desire of your eyes," we recall the words of Jesus to his disciples that "If anyone wishes to come after me, he must deny himself, and take up his cross and follow me" (Matt. 16:24, NASB). Ezekiel was way ahead of the moment then, when he continued to service the Lord, despite losing his beloved wife. He knew he would see her in heaven again someday.

When God breathes life into a valley of previously dry bones (in chapter 37), he shows Ezekiel that the remnant of Israel at the end of times will also partake of life and will join all believers in heaven one day.

In chapter 38, God gives him a vision of who the enemies will be at the end of times. He shares in receiving information privileged to other Biblical servants such as Daniel, Zechariah, and John, New Testament disciple of Jesus. Rewards from God for faithful servants should be nothing new for believers throughout the ages.

Amazing, Shocking, and Striking Visions

> 1:5: Within it there were figures resembling four living beings.

1:9b: Each went straight forward.

1:15: Now as I looked at the living beings, behold there was one wheel on the earth beside the living beings for each of the four of them.

2:2a: As he spoke to me, the Sprit entered into me and set me on my feet.

3:1a: Then He said to me, "Son of man, eat what you find. Eat this scroll."

3:3b: Then I ate it and it was as sweet as honey in my mouth. [John experienced this in his vision of the end of times (Rev. 10:9–10). Jeremiah had a similar experience (Jer. 15:16).]

8:10: So I entered and looked, and behold every form of creeping things and beasts and detestable things, with all the idols of the house of Israel, were carved on the wall all around. (A divine messenger takes Ezekiel in a vision to the temple and shows him graffiti written on the walls of the temple, showing the baseness of their thoughts and worship. Paul speaks of a similar baseness to come, which he describes in Romans 1:23–25.)

43:2b: His voice was like the sound of many waters; and the earth shone with his glory.

43:5a: The Spirit lifted me up and brought me into the inner court. [God lifts up the prophet both literally and figuratively speaking. A lesson for us is in times of deep distress, the Lord, whose love for us is as infinite as he himself, delights in lifting our spirits. When he does so, we praise him and return his love even more.]

43:6b,7a: I heard one speaking to me [from the house]. Son of man, this is...where I will dwell. (NASB)

Shocking Things Ezekiel Is Asked to Do In Order to Disseminate God's Message

1. In chapter 4, the prophet is asked to take a brick, inscribe on it a city, then set up miniature figures depicting a siege.2. Directly after the first assignment, he is to lie on his left side for 390 days, "equal to the number of years of their [Israel's] punishment." 3. Directly after the second assignment, he is to lie on his right side for forty days, representing forty years of punishment for Judah.4. Someone will make available a supply of water

and food sufficient for the duration of these demonstrations. 5. He is to bake his bread using human dung for a fire—to represent the unclean eating, God will reduce them to when they rebel.

Comparison: Ezekiel, Revelation, and a Personal Application

Ezekiel	Revelation	Application
Son of Man, feed your stomach… with this scroll, Then I ate it and it was sweet as honey (Ezek. 3:1–3, NASB).	I [John] took the little book… and ate… It was sweet as honey (10:10, NASB).	God's word is sweet to those who seek wisdom.
There was a man and a…measuring reed in his hand (40:3, NASB).	Then there was given me a measuring rod… and was told, "Get up and measure the temple…" (11:1, NASB).	We daily measure our steps knowing that our body is the temple of the Holy Spirit.

Ezekiel	Revelation	Application
Moreover I will send on you [Jerusalem] famine and wild beasts (5:17, NASB).	Authority was given to them over a fourth of the earth, to kill...with famine...and by wild beasts ["them" being Death and Hades, riding an ashen Horse] (Rev. 6:8b, the fourth of seven seals, NASB).	Pray your heart is in a good place as the Lamb sends out his angels riding their avenging steeds.

Study Questions

Choose one.

1. What is the meaning of Ezekiel's name? ("God is good"/"God strengthens") _____
2. From what Levitical priestly family did Ezekiel come? (Amalekite/Zadokite)_____
3. What was the name of Ezekiel's father? (Buzi/Jesse) _____
4. What was happening when Ezekiel's wife died? (Judah had just defeated a hated enemy/Judah was being carried off into captivity by the Babylonians.) _____

_____

5. How did God refer to Ezekiel's wife? ("the bride of your dreams/"the desire of your eyes") _____

_____

The Relevance of Ezekiel to Modern Christians

Ezekiel 38 and 39 mention a group of nations that will form a coalition during the tribulation period at the end of times. This coalition will include "Rosh, Meshech, and Tubal" (Ezek. 38:2). In addition, "Persia, Ethiopia and Put" (verse 5) along with "Gomer…[and] Beth-togarmah" (38:6).

In an argument that we may be living toward the end of times now, someone has noted that these Biblical places and names would correspond with modern Russia, Iran, Northern Sudan, Libya, Turkey et al. The same argument goes on to note that those countries not mentioned seem to fit the bill today as a list of places that either seek no association with the potentially aggressor nations or simply have too many problems of their own to be involved. The latter list would include Lebanon, Syria, Jordan, and Egypt.[5]

Ezekiel

I was by the River Chebar
In my thirtieth year
In bondage with Nebuchadnezzar—
A time of little cheer.

The word of God came to me
In a way I did not foresee
This would be the
Proof that God knew me.

He was making an impression
I would not soon forget.
I was frightened. Yes,
Yahweh definitely had my attention!

A storm came rumbling from the north,
A vision from God Almighty.
Bizarre, yet wonderful to see,
From the Father of Lights it came forth. [6]

Four living beings approaching
High up in the sky
But not too far for my purveying.
What striking sights I would espy!

Each being had four faces:
A man, a lion, bull, and eagle.
If you check Revelation four and seven
You will see these creatures again in heaven.

Other details also seen
In John's Revelation: eyes,
Flashes of lightning,
And wings on the cherubim.

Son of Buzi, Zadokite,
Of priestly family,
Who served during Babylon's might,
Transplanted into bleak captivity.

My wife, "The desire of your eyes,"
Who died in 588 BC
Could not be grieved, divine decree.[7]
They carried me off earlier, in 597 BC.

Like, later, God
Told John to eat
The scroll of heavenly vision.
At first, it was sweet.

Strange assignments, then, I received:
Like making a depiction of a siege,
Then lying on my side for months—
Acts not seen but yet believed:[8]

Ezekiel six: one through seven
Promises punishments for the leaven,
For the altars to other gods,
For the high places—not good odds.

If you are playing the idolatry game
Your days are numbered.
Yet, after idolatry's tamed
A remnant will be remembered.

Chapter eight finds me sitting
In my house with the elders,
When the likeness of a man appears.
The image of a man was fitting.

Stretching out my hand and seizing
Me, God's prophet, by a hair,
To the city of David transporting
Me, he shows me abominations there.

JAMES MANTHEY

Images of detestable creatures—
Graffiti on the wall
Of God's holy temple!
And that is not all.

Men inside facing east
And bowing to the ground
In an act of worship—more yeast—
Fear of the true God not found.

Chapter nine shows an avenging angel
Putting marks on the forehead of those offended.[9]
They will be saved; all others felled
For their defiance of a jealous "El."

In chapter twelve, to exile I go.
In sixteen, God remembers his covenant.
Nineteen laments the princes gone.
Throughout enumerated Judah's sins, a rant.

Designed to explain God's tough love?
The latter half of twenty-four—
Announcement of a decision from above:
My wife also will die, for…

The people then will see.
Their joy, their pride
Will also disappear
Just as their love for God had died.

Several nations then are judged,
Leading to the watchman
Of chapter thirty-three,
Whose job is to warn and coax each man.

Live in righteousness!
In the twelfth year of their exile,
Word comes: "Jerusalem falls!"
I speak again: my silence for a while…

Now broken! A token of God's plan
To restore a man
Like bones in the valley
Of thirty-seven—restored again with eyes that see!

The next two chapters have become the key
To understanding all prophecy.
More pieces to the puzzle—these
Applicable to Revelation, you see.

A man with measuring
Reed in his hand, another powerful image.
Our times are in his hands—
His reed, our lives, his gauge?

"God strengthens" all who read his book, [10]
Our future he'll predict.
If when we read, we will look
God's glory he'll depict.

Notes

1. NASB, p. 1207
2. Unger, p.378, says, "The 'bones' are the exiles. The valley, their dispersion. The graves, the death of their national life." If this vision does refer to the nation of Israel, or to the Jewish people themselves (throughout the ages), one cannot but wonder about the similarities between this and the holocaust of WWII, followed by their post-war nationhood. From rags to riches. From devastation, hopelessness, and despair to new life. Such will be the spiritual outcome for those Jews who find and accept Christ in their lifetimes. In addition, as the reader can see, I tell this poem in the first person singular, an interesting variation, exciting to write and read in this way.
3. Nelson, page 216
4. Unger, p.364
5. Don Stewart, Great Lakes Prophecy Conference, September 7, 2013, Calvary Chapel, Appleton, WI75: "Ten Signs That The End of Times Is Near." The text does not say that Ezekiel was afraid. Here, the poet puts himself in the place of the prophet and imagines what it may have been like. Therefore, some of the poem at this point becomes historical poetic fiction—an exception to the rule of attempting to render exactly what the text says.

6. James 1:17: "Every good gift and every perfect gift is from above and cometh down from the Father of Lights."
7. Ezekiel 24:16
8. Acts not seen by us, that is.
9. What their people were doing abhorred some Israelites. The latter did not participate. God would spare many of these in the coming punishment. Also, the Apostle Paul, in Romans 1:23, speaks of future people depraved in a similar way who, because of their wanton sin, will spend an eternity in hell.
10. Again, Ezekiel's name means "God strengthens," fitting for a man chosen to call people back to the source of their past strength and greatness, the Lord their God.

[note to layout: insert photo; centralize]

Daniel confounds the priests of Bel.

Daniel

ועתה   ואל־תחנוניו עבדך   תפלה אל־   אלהינו שמע

So now, our God, listen to the prayer of
Your servant and to his supplications.

—Daniel 9:17 (NASB)

ARRANGERS PLACED THE book of Daniel, along with
Lamentations, among the Ketuvim (the writings) instead
of the Nevi'im (the prophets) in the Hebrew Bible. His
name meaning, "God is my judge," Daniel was among what
the Babylonians must have considered the cream of the
crop of Hebrew society. He was a teenager in 605 BC when
he and three of his young friends began the next stage of
their lives, living under the thumb of Nebuchadnezzar and
the pagan people of Babylon. Later, when Babylon fell
to Persia, Daniel lived under the Persians. Through it all,

God's protective hand was there guiding and watching over his chosen leaders—a reward for their faithful witness. He would have been an octogenarian at the time of his great vision of the seventy weeks prophecy.[1]

In chapter nine, Daniel prays a prayer of remorse and confession for national sin, including a plea for repentance to the God for whom he has lived a life of service. Daniel's prayer was spurred on by his study of the book of Jeremiah (Dan. 9:2).[2]

Some have called Daniel the key to all biblical prophecy.[3]

In his vision to open up Revelation (1:13), John saw one "like a son of man." Daniel is privileged to describe one "like the son of God" (Dan. 3:25). This vision connects Daniel with John, Old Testament prophecy with the New, past Bible history with the future end of times, Old Testament believers with New (including us!).

Again, in chapter 9, Gabriel, heaven's archangel, describes Daniel as the one "highly esteemed" (9:23). Jesus and those who inhabit the throne room of God undoubtedly esteem any child of God whose faith constantly proves firm through the tests God sends. By the grace of God nothing could shake this blessed man's faith, come what may. Jesus once told Peter he would build his church upon such a faith (compared to a rock in the passage under scrutiny—Matt. 16:18). In a parable, elsewhere, Jesus spoke of the man who built his house upon a rock (Matt. 7:24–27).

No storm or even tidal wave of calamities in life could shake such a man's house. That house is the way we live our lives. Building our lives upon a rock, like Daniel did, results in a faith that, fueled by constant prayer and fellowship with the Father, fortified by a strong personal relationship of love and trust with the Father, Son, and Holy Spirit, remains faithful and true under fire. May we always strive for such a faith.

Some Observations

3:8–25: Many think the fourth person in the furnace to be the preincarnate Christ.[4]

Daniel got the position of third most powerful ruler as a reward for interpreting the inscription on Belshazzar's wall since Belshazzar was a co-regent.[5]

The interpretation mentioned weighing in a balance. Other places where Scripture mentions weighing in a balance include Job 31:6, Psalm 62:9, Proverbs 16:2.

The lions' den incident took place under Darius, the Mede. Daniel was an old man then—eighty years old. "This is a vision of the second advent of Christ" (Dan. 7:9–14); "The saints who possess the kingdom are the Jewish remnant who survived the tribulation" (Dan. 7:15–28).[6]

In Chapter 9, we find Daniel's prayer of repentance and request for forgiveness, starts out in the spirit of a Davidic

Psalm—words from the heart, emanating from a man of God after God's own heart (in the spirit of King David). Daniel realizes, therefore, that the time of captivity is ending soon. In the midst of his discourse, he focuses on the theme of shame—how he, Judah, including Jerusalem, and "all Israel" (9:7 ff.), "both near and far in all the countries where you have scattered us," have now experienced "open shame" (Dan. 9:8). When Daniel spoke of shame, he was touching on a theme other prophets also mentioned. Jeremiah, for example, the inspiration of Daniel (who was mentioned in Daniel 9:2), had said, "How great is our shame." Earlier, in Jeremiah 6:15, the prophet had to admit: "They [God's people] have no shame." Jeremiah 3:25 (NASB) said, "Let us lie down in our shame and let our humiliation cover us." We have noted before how the peculiar calling of Hosea, the command he received from God to marry a harlot, was all about the shame God's people had brought upon themselves.

On a different note, the genre or style of literature that Daniel is written in is predominantly narrative, historical narrative. It is the reason arrangers listed Daniel among the "writings" rather than the "prophets" in the Hebrew Bible. This is different from most of the other prophets.

This historical account includes apocalyptic literature— prophecies about the end of times as well as predictions of other future events. This factual account of faithfulness, at times literally in the teeth (lions' den) of all odds, contains several historical accounts within one entirely historical account, all classics: the three men in the fiery furnace, Belshazzar and the writing on the wall, Daniel in the lions' den, interpretation of visions—the great statue, the great tree, the goat and the ram.

Comparison: Daniel, Revelation, and a Personal Application

Daniel	Revelation	Application
"…Test your servants for ten days. Let us be given…vegetables… (1:12, NASB).	"You are about to suffer…prison, that you may betested, and for ten days you will have tribulation" (2:10, ESV).	"Blessed is the man who remains steadfast under trial, for when he has stood the test he will receive the crown of life" (James 1:12, ESV).
"As I looked, thrones were placed and the Ancient of Days took His seat" (7:9, ESV)	"Then I saw thrones and seated on them were those to whom authority to judge was committed" (20:4, ESV).	All believers are this moment part of a royal priesthood. (1 Pet. 2:9 ff.)

Daniel	Revelation	Application
"And as I looked the Beast was killed… and given over to be burned with fire" (7:11, ESV).	"And the beast was captured, and with it the false prophet; these two were thrown alive into the lake of fire" (19:20, ESV).	Torment awaits those who turn away from God.
"A thousand thousands Served Him, and ten thousand times ten thousand. The court sat in judgment and the books were opened" (7:10, ESV).	"The dead… great and… small, standing before the throne, and books were opened" (20:12, NASB).	Through Christ our names too will be found in the Book of Life.

Study Questions

Choose one.

1. In what season of his life was Daniel when Babylon took him captive? (Early childhood/Probably a teen)

    _____

2. What is a good estimate for the year of Daniel's captivity? (705 BC /605 BC) _____

3. Who were the two peoples that Daniel served? Choose two. (Egyptians, Persians, Greeks, Babylonians) The _____ and the _____ _____.

4. In what chapter does Daniel realize the sins of his people and then pray for forgiveness? (Chapter 1/Chapter 9) _____

5. What Old Testament prophet spurred Daniel on to remorse and confession of sins for his people? (Ezekiel/ Jeremiah) _____

_____

How Daniel Speaks to Us Yet Today

We all feel a special blessing when a solid man of God comes on the scene, someone who is greatly gifted and who stays faithful to the Lord. Charles Stanley continues to lead people to the Savior through a gifted paternal type of fireside chat. Often, Charles is sitting down after the fashion of a rabbi—as Jesus often was recorded doing. Modern technology has captured Billy Graham's evangelistic fire for all times in classic remakes of the Billy Graham Crusades, beginning in the fifties and continuing well into the new millennium. Any pastor or sermon that calls us to repentance and seeks a renewal of commitment and faith is calling after a fashion reminiscent of Daniel. Christians yet today attempt to replicate the "Daniel Diet" of fruit, vegetables, and water. Those champions of the reformation—John Wycliffe, John Huss, and Martin Luther—captured the unswerving faithfulness to stand by what you believe, despite the consequences. Using your position in high places to influence the culture in which you live, turning hearts toward your Lord and Maker, once again reminds us of the Reverend Billy Graham, not to mention the earlier Peter Marshall. With the book of Revelation and the end of times on the lips and minds of so many Christians, we cannot help but feel God speaking through Daniel yet today. Some people refer to Daniel as the "key to all interpretation of the end of times."[9]

We thank God for men like Daniel. We pray that his life and words may inspire us all to live God-pleasing lives. May the Holy Spirit Himself, in the spirit of Daniel, move us to be the best we can for the Lord within the context of the times and world in which we live.

Daniel

"God is my judge"
In Godly devotion would not budge
When the Lord came calling
With Jerusalem falling.

Taken in the first wave
Of 605 BC
He became a model
Of faith—to follow.

Hananiah, Mishael and Azariah,[10]
Three of Daniel's young friends—
They also forced to go
As part of Nebuchadnezzar's show.

These four they would test,
Requesting a kosher diet.
Despite the king's insistence
They obtained their request.

For God gives protection
To those he loves.
We see it time and again
In the one "highly esteemed" from above.[11]

The lives of the special three
Rested in God's mercy.
When thrown into the fire
Nothing ill transpired.

The king's order?
"Turn up the heat."
So hot was the fire
That the captors expired.

The king himself saw
A fourth "man" inside.
A preincarnate visit?
A theophany? The Christ?

The king acknowledged God,
A fact soon repeated
But not enough for salvation,
As with Jonah's Assyrian nation.

After Nebuchadnezzar,
Then Belshazzar,
After the statue and great tree
Then "Mene, mene, tekel, parsin"[12]

"God is my judge" next spent a night
With lions.
Darius, the Mede's, turn
To proclaim God "king."

Another vision—
This time four beasts:
The "Ancient of Days" reigns—
"The Son of Man" co-reigns.

This latter vision
Is an expression
(I think it is true)
Of Psalm 2—

Where the Father of all
Declares his "decree:"
The nations shall be his inheritance,
At end-times, and thence.

More visions follow.
On to chapter nine.
Here Daniel, awakened by Jeremiah,[13]
Realizes freedom is nigh—

Then before the coming Messiah.
There will be a final
Remnant of Jews,
An end to their blues

After seventy "weeks."[14]
More visions for the far future
Came to elder Daniel—
The full meaning sealed,

In "Revelation" revealed.
Seven and sixty-two
The time until the temple is rebuilt
Then the time until Christ comes true,[15]

Week sixty-nine to seventy
A "week" that has been postponed.
Jerusalem to be restored,
Some Jews will trust our Lord.[16]

Notes

1. Nelson, 167
2. Nelson, 168
3. Unger, 382 says, "It's the key to all Biblical prophecy: Jesus's great Olivet Discourse (Matthew 24–25; Mark 13, Luke 21), as well as 2 Thess. 2 and Revelation. Themes of NT prophecy that are revealed here include the manifestation of the antichrist, the Great Tribulation, the second advent of the Messiah, the times of the Gentiles; resurrections and judgments are all treated in Daniel."
4. Ibid., 386
5. Ibid., 388
6. Ibid., 390
7. Ibid., 386
8. Ibid., 388
9. Go to this website: www.NTEB.org *Now The End Begins* and read the article on "Understanding the Prophecy of Daniel's Seventy Weeks" (re: Dan. 9:2 and Dan. 9:24–27). Do not skip the link to another article entitled "The Evils and Errors of Replacement Theology."
10. Renamed Shadrach, Meshach, and Abednego by the king's commander of officials (Dan. 1:7). On Peter Marshall: May 27, 1902–January 26, 1949 was a Scots-American preacher, pastor of the New York Avenue

Presbyterian Church in Washington, DC, and twice appointed as chaplain of the United States Senate, from Wikipedia, the online encyclopedia

11. "For you are highly esteemed" were the words of Gabriel to Daniel in Daniel 9:23.

12. The writing on the wall for Belshazzar and the Babylonians who were overthrown that very night. Thus began the rule of Darius the Mede or Darius the Persian.

13. Having read and pondered Jeremiah 29:10

14. Where scholars take "weeks" in Daniel to mean seven times seventy years. They would understand seventy of these "weeks", therefore, to mean 490 years.

15. *Now The End Begins* (a website), the article on "Understanding the Prophecy of Daniel's Seventy Weeks" (re: Dan. 9:2 and Dan. 9:24–27). Do not skip the link to another article entitled "The Evils and Errors of Replacement Theology."

16. Ibid.

[note to layout: insert photo; centralize]

Hosea, at God's command, marries Gomer, a prostitute, to portray the sins and hoped for repentance theLord seeks from those He loves.

Hosea

דברי   הושע ־ אל היה אשר יהוה ־

The word of the Lord which came to Hosea.

—Hosea 1:1a (NASB)

Points of Interest in Hosea

HOSEA, SON OF Beeri, served about the middle of the eighth century BC, during or just after the ministry of Amos. He may have prophesied for about thirty-eight years, as the final years of the northern kingdom ended. "While Amos credited an unnamed enemy with being poised to end the northern kingdom, Hosea identifies the enemy as Assyria." In the tumultuous last years of the kingdom, this prophet (the only writing prophet from the north) would have experienced six kings in a twenty-five-year period: Zechariah, Shallum, Pekahiah, and Pekah, their successor having murdered them while in office.[1]

The expressions of God's love for his people in the midst of his denunciation for their sins reminds of Jesus's pre-Passion Week mourning for Jerusalem: "Jerusalem, Jerusalem, who kills the prophets and stones those who are sent to her! How often I wanted to gather your children together, the way a hen gathers her chicks under her wings, and you were unwilling" (Matt. 23:37, NASB). It is amazing that God loves us, even in the midst of our sins, in spite our sins. When we turn to Christ, God sees us differently. Then we become justified. If we continue by God's help to work out our salvation, we become sanctified. Israel, under Hosea, was not yet turning from their sins.

In the movie *It's a Wonderful Life*, George (Jimmie Stewart) gets to see what his beloved city and townspeople would be like without him.[2]

Allow for a moment that George could represent the prophet. Mr. Potter, the greedy, wicked banker, represents the king of Israel. The town, without George, turned into Pottersville, a wicked place ruled by greed, vice, hatred, murder. Transfer the analogy to Hosea.

With the prophet still in the picture, there was hope for the town, hope for the fruits of the Spirit ("But the fruit of the spirit is: love, joy, peace, patience, kindness, goodness, faithfulness, gentleness, self-control; against such things there is no law" [Gal. 5:22–23, NASB].) The Lord's prophets all made a difference even when the majority of the people did not listen. They represented hope, hope that God's people would return to righteousness. There also must have been hope for the truly righteous that the political climate of wickedness would one day change. Habakkuk, in his time became an effective mouthpiece for the latter people.

"When Israel was a youth, I loved him" (Hosea 11:1a, NASB). reminds me of Mom when we were kids and had been behaving badly. Mom could be very direct. She would say words to the effect, "Sometimes the way you kids behave I feel as though I like you better when you are sleeping." Ouch. Tough love from either our earthly parents or our heavenly one can sting. The hurt, however, goes away when we realize they love us more than we will ever be able to understand. In God's case, He loved us so much he sacrificed his son who, in turn, willingly went to the cross, died, rose again, and ascended on high—all for us.

God travels back and forth in Hosea between righteous anger, promises of punishment, and tender cajoling. This consistently inconsistent behavior intends to mirror Israel's constant wavering in their devotion to their God and Heavenly Father, Yahweh.

In Hosea 12:1, the "east wind" recalls connotations of evil associated with the east in the Bible. Other examples include God placing a cherubim and a rotating flaming sword on the east side of Eden after driving out His unfaithful and sinful creatures, Adam and Eve. Cain, after his curse and branding, heads east to find a life, having failed to repent of his sin of murder.

Ishmael and Hagar were sent east after their banishment, by Abraham at Sarah's request. The entrance to the tabernacle was at the east end, from where one would approach more closely to God, the Holy Place and the Most Holy Place.[3]

Asking a prophet, God's servant, to marry a harlot seems a horrible thing. Yet difficult situations often called for difficult appeals from God to his messengers. The Lord our God, after In sports, they say that the best referees, the best umpires, the best line judges are the ones who do their job and yet kind of blend into the game in the background. Out of all the prophets you can study, we can see the personalities of these men pretty clearly. With Hosea, his personality kind of melts into the background as he becomes more purely the mouthpiece of God. More than any other prophet, perhaps, it is as though God is speaking through Hosea and not Hosea speaking for God. To undergo heartbreak as Hosea did with his unfaithful wife must have been an extremely humbling and humiliating thing. "Blessed are the poor in spirit, for theirs is the kingdom of Heaven" (Matt. 5:3, NASB). Undoubtedly this was what helped make him such a perfect vessel for God's Word to His people, both to his contemporaries and to people throughout all times, including to us.

Three-Point Comparison: Hosea, Revelation, And Personal Application

Hosea	Revelation	Application
Hosea 9:10 (Israel used to bring joy to God's heart; also Hosea 12:6)	Revelation 2:4 (Ephesus has forgotten its first love).	Seek a revival, a restoration of our joy in Christ's return—a return, on our part, to a loving faith that binds us to God.
Hosea 10:8b, NASB "Then they will say to the mountains: 'Cover us' and to the hills: 'Fall on us.'"	Revelation 6:16, NASB Same as Hosea, plus, "Fall on us and hide us from him who sits on the throne and from the wrath of the Lamb."	If we love God and obey his laws, we will never have to fear his punishment.

Hosea	Revelation	Application
Hosea 14:1 says, "Return"—an oft-repeated theme in Hosea.[5]	Revelation 4:1 and Revelation 22:17–21 says, "Come."	When we stay faithful to God and his Word, the Lord will not have to say "come," much less "return," as we are already right there with him.
Hosea 14:5–7 Israel will flourish under God's blessing.	Revelation 7:1–8 (A remnant from the twelve tribes will be saved.)	God will save a remnant from Israel. Jew and Gentile alike, however, must trust in the Lord.

Study Questions

Choose one.

1. Who was the father of Hosea? (Buzi/Beeri) _____
    _____

2. When did Hosea serve? (Sixth century BC /Eighth century BC) _____

3. What was the name of Hosea's wife? (Rachel/Gomer)
    _____

4. What is distinctive about Hosea among other writing prophets? (He was a Hebrew convert./ He was asked to marry a harlot to dramatize in real life the spoiled relationship between God and His people.)
5. What was going on the in the northern kingdom during Hosea's tenure as prophet? (There was murder and intrigue in high places resulting in the death of several kings./ There was peace and uninterrupted prosperity.)

The Relevance of Hosea Today

Like Gomer, America today seems to be prostituting itself. Israel did it by worshipping foreign gods. We are doing it at the altar of political correctness. Just as Satan who goes about like a roaring lion seeking whom he may devour, enemies of Christianity, God and Christ are continuously on the prowl. Almost daily, we hear of another state passing laws allowing same-sex marriage. The pro-abortion laws have been on the books since the *Roe v. Wade* decision in 1973. Some of Christianity's best known evangelists and preachers are showing signs of watering down the Bible, soft pedaling mention of Jesus and of God the Father, in the attempt to warm up to Islam (the "Chrislam" movement) so as to create unity and harmony. Up above, the Lord watches in sorrow, as his people stand idly by, dumb as a sheep before its shearers, tragically silent at a time when God is looking for boldness and a defense of righteousness.

Jesus commanded us to be salt and light in the world (in Matthew 5, from the Sermon on the Mount). Salt, because the world tends toward bad taste when it comes to following God's will; light, because the world loves darkness. First John 1 warns us that anyone who calls himself Christian is a liar if he continues to walk in darkness. Not to speak up on issues of morality results in sins of omission—just as punishable, by God's standards, as sins of commission. Hosea, contrasting with the fiery warnings of Amos, extends the Lord's loving and compassionate call to repentance to all who would listen. The Lord is slow to anger, abounding in love, and will go to any means to bring us back. Offering his only begotten Son, Jesus Christ, on a Roman cross was the ultimate sacrifice, the culmination of the multiple millennium protoevangelium plan of salvation, to call us back home. Jesus told the parable of the prodigal son to personalize God's forgiveness and compassion. The Lord works through Hosea yet today, to remind us of our heritage as the bride of Christ. Like Gomer, we too have been like a harlot in pursuit of other "lovers" (interests and fleshly idols). Yet God, like Hosea, is waiting for us to return home to Him.

People often do not well receive prophets, or anyone, really, who shares the "good news." Yet God wants his messengers to deliver the message despite the reception. Jesus told the seventy He sent out, that if they experienced rejection, to wipe the dust off their feet and go on to the next place. We must still do the same.

In Hosea's case, for us it would have been a hard sell. God had to go to drastic means to get the people's attention. Yet someone has said, "One of the most unloving things a Christian could conceive of would be to not tell people of their need for a Savior."[6]

Hosea

Hosea, son of Beeri,
Goes back to Jeroboam,
To Judah's: Uzziah, Jotham,
Ahaz, and Hezekiah.

The Lord came to his prophet,
A strange hurtful command:
"Take to wife a harlot
Who reflects the sins of the land."

Some say this never happened.
Higher critics make this claim.
To question God's clear statements
Is to stain God's holy name.

Gomer bears a son.
"Jezreel," his name—
A public reflection of
A valley's bloody shame.

Warnings for the north,
Ten tribes of Israel.
The avenger bears a torch
For the day when they will fall.

"Lo-Ruhamah," the female next child,
Meaning, "My compassion is spent,"
Israel's idolatry was wild.
The warning went unheeded, though sent.

A final son, "Lo Ammi,"
For you are not my kin.
From child to child a progression
Showing divine displeasure at sin.[7]

Gomer, the harlot,
God-approved wife of a prophet
Is called to repent
And is told that

Her former trappings:
Which spoke of wages
Received from sinning
Would be stripped away in stages.

Just like Israel's past devotion
To the Baals and other false beings
Would provoke no small demonstration
Of his wrath, meant for their seeing.

Throughout the unraveling
Of this divine plot
Appears God's mercy, a thing
Designed to blot

Out their sins, restore:
This a coaxing, for those straying,
To make them want more—
God's mercy then staying.

Notes

1. NASB, 1250–1251 passim
2. Liberty Films, 1946, directed by Frank Capra, starring James Stewart and Donna Reed
3. Wayne Barber, Eddie Rasnake, Richard Shepherd, *Life Principles for Worship From the Tabernacle* (Chattanooga, Tennessee: AMG Publishers, 2001), 40. One caveat here would be that others have found evidence of good things coming from the east such as the wise men with their gifts from the Christmas story.
4. NASB, 1250
5. Wayne Barber, Eddie Rasnake, Richard Shepherd, *Life Principles From the Prophets of the Old Testament* (AMG Publishers, 1999), 73, where Barber et al note that the Hebrew word (*shuwb*), "return," occurs twenty-two times in Hosea.
6. Chris Quintana, speaker at the Great Lakes Prophecy Conference, Calvary Chapel, Appleton, Wisconsin, September 7, 2013. Topic: "Modern Israel."
7. Wayne Barber, Eddie Rasnake, Richard Shepherd

[note to layout: insert photo; centralize]

The prophet Joel, James Tissot, 1888:
A plague of locusts awaits the ungodly.

Joel

דבר־יהוה   ־פתואל   בן יואל ־ אל היה אשר

The word of the Lord that came
to Joel, the son of Pethuel.

—Joel 1:1 (NASB)

JOEL'S NAME MEANS "Yahweh is God." Scholars are not in agreement with when Joel lived since he gives no clue in the book of prophecy bearing his name. The choices are post-exilic (the more modern view) and about 800 BC.[1]

From Joel's description of Jerusalem's destruction, it is possible he was a citizen there. Because of the detailed description of that city's destruction in 586 BC, preceded by the first deportation to Babylonian captivity (605 BC), Joel's gifts of prophecy would be diminished had he actually reported firsthand his description of post-destruction Jerusalem. The conservative view, however, is that his powers were much more impressive, due to the vision he received as a contemporary of Isaiah, anywhere from 800 BC on.[2]

Because of his mention of priestly information, many have thought Joel a priest. In that case, we could associate him with the likes of other prophet/priests: Samuel, Jeremiah, Ezekiel, and Zechariah.

When Joel begins talking about the "Day of the Lord" and the end of times in chapter two, he precedes Jesus's description of the end of times in Matthew 24. Joel emphasized the locust attack and then went into other details. Jesus enumerated several events in His own right. Joel's call to repentance at chapter 2:12 ff. was designed to make people want to find God and cling to the promises. Jesus designed His parables, such as those recounted in Matthew 13, make people yearn for the kingdom and for eternal fellowship with Him. Allow Joel to put the fear of God in your heart. Then when news of what awaits an unbelieving world has sunk in and broken you down, let his call to repentance build you up, such as the deliverance promised, for example, at Joel 2:18 ff. The "broken and contrite heart" of Psalm 51:17, in a similar spirit, will then lead to the delight of the Lord described in Psalm 51:19.

Themes in Joel

Judgment and destruction are coming: The book opens with the announcement of a coming plague of locusts. Joel, God's messenger, might remind Americans of a past national messenger, Paul Revere, who rode to Lexington to warn leaders of the approach of the British. In that sense, then, Joel's warning is meant to wake Israel up to the fact of their sins (eg, drunkenness: 1:5).

God's people need to confess and repent of their sins: They have been too fond of wine (1:5) for one.

The prophet is a social/religious gadfly called to move people to action: God's people need no spurring on to action except when their inaction or lethargy has become a sin in God's eyes. The Lord would call Haggai and Zechariah to spur Israel to rebuild God's temple after the return from Babylon. God chose Joel to lead the people to repent (1:13–14) for "Who knows whether He will not turn and relent and leave [instead of destruction] a blessing behind Him" (2:14, NASB).

The natural destruction (by locusts) mentioned in chapter 1 was either symbolic or an actual punishment. The message serves as precursor to the human destruction that will occur on "the day of the lord": The "Day of the Lord" is a theme mentioned throughout Scripture: Amos 5:18–20;[3] Isaiah 13:6, 9; Jeremiah 46:10; Zephaniah 1:7, 14–16; 2

Peter 3:10 (quoting Joel during his Pentecost sermon that led to the three thousand conversion); and 1 Thessalonians 5:2.

Three-Point Comparison: Joel, Revelation, and a Personal Application

Joel	Revelation	Application
Its teeth are the teeth of a lion [army of locusts] (1:6, NASB)	Their teeth were like the teeth of lions (9:8, NASB).	It is a dreadful thing to fall into the hands of an angry God (words of Jonathan Edwards).[4]
Their (the locusts') appearance is like the appearance of horses. (2:4, NASB)	The appearance of the locusts was like horses prepared for battle (9:7, NASB)	When locusts look like angry horses, God's people will either be safe in heaven or watching unafraid from a earthly vantage point that allows them to see through the eyes of faith.

Study Questions

Choose one.

1. What is the meaning of Joel's name? (Yahweh is God/ Yahweh is good) _____
2. What are two possibilities for when Joel lived? (Post-exilic/800 BC or 1200 BC/ 605 BC) _____
   _____or _____
3. What other occupation do some scholars think Joel may have had? (Shepherd/Priest) _____
   _____ Why? (He has many metaphors for sheep/He shows an intimate knowledge of priestly functions) _____
   _____
4. What is one strong theme in Joel? (The coming judgment/God is not merciful) _____
   _____
5. What is the plague most often associated with Joel? (Water turned to blood/Locusts) _____
   _____

The Relevance of Joel in Our Day and Age

The call to sobriety in Joel applies perfectly to our society today, which loves its alcohol as is proven by the high number of alcoholics. How many families has alcohol abuse destroyed? How many more abuses will occur? How many more offences against humanity will be committed? How many more fatal accidents caused? How many more marriages brought to an end? What about those locusts?

The 1937 award-winning movie, *The Good Earth*, set in China, shows in graphic detail what an attack of locusts might look like, including the one at the end of time. We can best appreciate the fearful sight of gnawing, swarming, creeping, and stripping locusts from the vantage point of a farmer who helplessly watches his crops being vaporized before his very eyes. We also will see our livelihood, our hopes, our dreams dissolve before our view when we turn from God and ignore His warnings. Joel presents a clarion call to repentance. The prophet almost screams at his listeners, God's people, to turn from sin.

What sin plagues us most? What sin most brings our city, state, and country under the avenging eye of a jealous and righteous judge? How about the arrogance of rulers leading their people astray, like sheep over the cliff, away from God? How does God view judges and rulers who call good "bad" and bad "good?" Psalm 2:4 says it well: "He who sits in the heavens laughs, the Lord scoffs at him." The call to repentance for rulers in verses ten to twelve of the same psalm (2) sheds more light: "Now, therefore, O kings, show discernment; take warning, O judges of the earth. Worship the Lord with reverence and rejoice with trembling. Do homage to the Son that He not become angry, and you perish in the way."

Joel

Pethuel had a son
Named "Yahweh is God,"
"Joel's" meaning—
The spirit already intervening

In the life of one
Called to sound a warning
Of god's impending wrath
On those who have left the path.

Gnawing, swarming, creeping, stripping
Locusts are coming.
Drunkards weeping,
Mockers agreeing.

Tissot has depicted
A prophet downcast
Who sees a punishment
The Lord intends

For people prone to sin.
As in Samuel, Ezekiel,
Jeremiah, and Zechariah—
A priestly hint

God weaves throughout.
The locusts are coming.
Their sound is like a humming,
In the sky all about.

The day of the Lord is near!
A very Biblical theme,
The teeth of one: six's locust
Like a lion's, they seem!

Watch *The Good Earth*,
Worthy reader,
And see what we mean, the vision—equine
Of 2:4's line.

Psalm two: six to nine comes to mind
At the mention of Zion's holy mountain:
"Then said he to me,
Today I have made a decree.

As for me
I have installed my king
Upon Zion's holy hill
For anything; just ask of me."

Before them a fire,
Behind them a flame,⁵
Efforts of farmers to save?
Watch *The Good Earth* (again).

As always, amidst the dire doom,
A light to ease the gloom
Streams into the room
Springing up like heavenly mushrooms:

The Lord will be zealous.
Yet, He'll have pity on us.
Psalm one o three: nine and ten—
A salve comes to mind again.

Music to the ears
Of the humble.
A divine finger
To dry our tears.

Mercy to all through the years.
Calm your fears.
You will be full again:
Beast, land, and men.

Praise the name of
The Lord your God.
Visions and dreams for old men and young.
Prophecy for sons, daughters—young.

Yet, judgment and death in the long run—
Joy for believers, wickedness done.
Chastisement for Judah:
Sold for gold to another.

Though sun and moon grow dim,
Stars losing their shine,
We will find a spring in heaven,
Reviewed in Psalm forty-six: four again.

Fortunes go high and low
For those who cannot stay true.
This is a recurring clue
In the prophets who serve below.

Notes

1. Unger, 403
2. Nelson, 329
3. Probably "the earliest mention": Ibid., 172
4. Jonathan Edwards (October 5, 1703–March 22, 1758) was a Christian preacher, philosopher, and theologian. Edwards "is widely acknowledged to be America's most important and original philosophical theologian," (from Wikipedia, the electronic encyclopedia.)
5. Joel 2:3 (NASB) which repeats the same idea in a more poetic form: "The land is like the Garden of Eden before them but a desolate wilderness behind them…"

[note to layout: insert photo; centralize]

Amos the lowly shepherd, called to minister to a people blinded by pride. God calls us as well to be humble followers of His will.

Amos

מחמס   בושה תכסך יעקב אחיך   לולם ונכרת

The words of Amos, who was among the
sheepherders from Tekoa, which he envisioned
in visions concerning Israel in the days of Uzziah
king of Judah [the opening words go on to say].

—Amos 1:1 (NASB)

AMOS, IN CONTRAST to Isaiah's rumored derivation from
royal ancestry, was a simple shepherd from Tekoa, a hilly
area about ten miles south of Jerusalem. Just as Amos's
ministry ended, that of Isaiah, in fact, would begin. Where
Isaiah's beginning coincided with the death of King Uzziah
(king of Judah), Amos was the main prophet during the
latter's period of rule (765–750 BC). These were heady days,
especially for the more materially blessed of God's people.

Yet instead of giving God the glory and holding to God's Word in humility, there was corruption and idolatry everywhere. To this morally sick people and time, God called another prophet (besides Hosea who is from the same time) to expose their sin, leading them to repentance.[1]

We find shepherds in the story of the Savior's first advent where lowly shepherds were among the first to hear the gospel good news of the Messiah's arrival. Having received the message, they went to the city of David to see if it was true. The angels were correct! Luke 2:17 says, "When they had seen this, they made known the statement which had been told them about this Child." God privileged the shepherds from the Christmas story to share an entirely joyous message. Amos also faithfully conveyed the entire anointed message God gave him. Yet his words, like those of all the prophets, were a mixture of good and bad. Both warning and encouragement, judgment and mercy, punishment and restoration are in store for God's chosen people from whom the Savior would derive. Tough love was emanating from a jealous and Holy Father for the remnant—seed of the coming Promised One. Did not Jesus, our great High Priest, King, and, most fittingly for this study, Prophet par excellence, include all these message elements? It does not take much thought to recall instances from the Gospel accounts of each, ie, instances where Jesus gave warning and encouragement, judgment and mercy, punishment yet also restoration.

Three-Point Comparison: Amos, Revelation, and a Personal Application

Amos	Revelation	Application
"For those who turn into wormwood and cast righteousness down to the earth." (5:7, NASB)	"A great star fell.. The name of the star is called Wormwood. Many men died from the waters." (8:10b–11, NASB)	In Rev. 3:16, the justice warns the church in Laodicea that they will be "spit out" for being "lukewarm"; how much will the Lord spit out those who pervert righteousness.
"Will not the day of the Lord be darkness instead of light?" (5:20a NASB)	"A third of the sun and a third of the moon and a third of the stars were struck so that a third of them would be darkened." (8:12, NASB)	The world loves darkness. Therefore, when natural light begins to disappear, they will be in their natural element.

Study Questions

Choose one.

1. What was the calling of Amos before he became a prophet? (Priest/Shepherd) _____

2. What was the time of Amos? (Early tenth century BC/ latter eighth century BC) _____
    _____

3. Who was king during Amos's years of service to the Lord? (Jeroboam/Uzziah) _____
    _____

4. What were things like in Israel during Amos's watch? (Assyria was destroying them /the people were enjoying great prosperity) _____
    _____

5. What was the main spiritual problem the people had? (Corruption and idolatry/No attention to sacrifices)
    _____

What Amos Means to the Believer Today

Although there is no immediate joy for the believer in news of the wicked's demise, take comfort in knowing that God will spare you from the punishment of unbelief. This does not mean that life will be a bed of roses for a Christian. We know all too well that it is not. Yet at worst, the bad things that happen to God's people more often result in a testing of our faith and strengthening of the relationship with our Lord and Savior.

That high-ranking officials warned Amos (Amaziah, the priest, in chapter 7:12) for speaking the truth should not surprise us. Elijah was constantly under threat from Ahab and Jezebel. An entire Syrian army surrounded Elisha. The people of Jerusalem, under order from their king, beat God's prophet, put him in chains, threw him into a muddy cistern, and almost left him for dead. The wicked never want to hear that what they are doing is wrong. We have a saying for such people: there are none so blind as those who will not see. Contemporary Christians in our country are receiving warnings from several quarters about preaching boldly and publicly of Christ. The catchwords of today's stifling politically correct atmosphere warns, "Separation of church and state. Cease and desist or be punished."

What should be our response? Like Amos, we must be bold where we can: "I am not a prophet. Yet the Lord said to me: 'Go prophesy to my people.'" Jesus, Son of God himself, has given us the Great Commission: "Go ye, therefore, and make disciples of all nations" (Matt. 28:19, NASB).

Amos

Amos, a lowly shepherd,
Called by God through visions,
Derived from hilly Tekoah,
Eleven miles south of Jerusalem.

This divine spokesman
Contrasts interestingly
With Isaiah who followed him
In time, not ancestry.

Isaiah had royal connections.
Amos, from common clay.
Amos, the prophet for King Uzziah.
For the former, the king was away.[2]

"Justice turned to wormwood,
Righteousness cast down."
With hearts misplaced
Could God do other than frown?

What words of fire
From a mere shepherd,
Chosen to conspire
With an angry Lord!

Warnings go out from Zion:
The Lord shouting like a lion.
"Beware Damascus, Hazael,
Palace where Ben-Hadad dwells.

Gaza, then, and Ashdod,
Ashkelon and Ekron—
Philistines' top four cities, devoid of God.
Others: Edom and Ammon."

Edom's sentence we find
In Amos one, verse eleven
(As in Psalm 137 and seven):
"Repay them in kind."

Judges and princes alike,
Marked for destruction.
Could this be right?
Even Judah in desolation?

Yes! Their atrocities many:
Righteous betrayed.
Poor turned aside.
The wicked are plenty.

Amaziah's warning
For Amos, the true:
A false prophet's mourning
For a true prophet's truth.

Like words from Ben-Hur:[3]
"Row well and live,"
"Seek me and live!"
Will the humble concur?

Chapter five's lamentation
For a nation in need—
Giving in to temptation,
Cruelty, and greed.

"Seek good, not evil,
That you may live":
A plea all for naught
If the people don't give

Heed to the voice from above.
Feast days and offerings,
Sacred assemblies
Bring only sufferings

For heavenly hosts.
They go through the motions
Of righteous worship.
The rich luxuriate,

God's truth not in grip
Brings to mind James five:
"Weep and howl you rich;
Wealth a testimony against you.

You've killed the just."
My patience is through.
What's lacking is justice
And righteousness too.

Then visions ensue:
Locusts and fire.
God's punishment true?
No. He relents at the wire.

Visions continue.
The Lord is on a roll.
A plumb line, a wall—
Is Israel on parole?

To Amaziah's warning—
Amos' reply:
"You shall be in mourning—
Wife ravished; kids die."

Final sight? A basket of fruit.
No mercy this time:
Restoration of truth,
This justice mine (says the Lord).

In the end, however,
When all is said and done
God's people will weather
The storm. Their fortunes, turned.

Notes

1. Unger, 407
2. King Uzziah died at the beginning of Isaiah's reign. Amos, instead, served during Uzziah's best years— before he fell from grace at the end of his reign.
3. *Ben-Hur*, 1959 film, directed by William Wyler, produced by Sam Zimbalist, a Metro-Goldwyn-Mayer film, starring Charlton Heston, adapted from Lew Wallace's 1880 novel: *Ben Hur: A Tale of the Christ*.

[note to layout: insert photo; centralize]

A message of woe for the Edomites.

Obadiah

מחמס   בושה תכסך יעקב אחיך   לולם ונכרת

[To Edom] Because of the violence to your
brother Jacob, you will be covered with
shame, and you will be cut off forever.

—Obadiah 1:10 (NASB)

HIS NAME MEANS "servant of the Lord." Obadiah's is the
shortest prophecy and book of the Old Testament. His is
also possibly the oldest of the prophetic books, other than
Samuel. Many want to date him shortly after Jerusalem's
fall in 586 BC. Internal evidence, however (centering around
the relevancy of Edom; eg, 2 Kings 8:20–22 and 2 Chron.
21:8–10), make the reign of Jehoram (c.848–841 BC) the
more likely date for "the servant of the Lord."[1]

We cannot identify Obadiah with any of the twelve or so others by the same name in the Old Testament.[2]

If it is true Obadiah is one of the oldest of the prophetic books, then his voice represents a voice of wisdom from the past. We would do well, as in—it would be wise to pay heed to such a voice. Obadiah teaches us that when we are in tune with God's will, he may use us to bring clarity and closure to a situation that has been hanging over the head of God's people for a long time. Keep your ear to the ground: Ask God for His blessing in establishing a tight vertical relationship between you and your God and Redeemer. Then you can reach out in the horizontal and serve your fellow man with words of comfort. The comfort can still derive from knowing that God has never ceased from dealing with our enemies. His angels guard and protect us at all times.

On the other hand, Jesus has taught us not to seek revenge, much less take joy in the demise of those who are against us. Instead, "Vengeance is mine; I will repay," says the Lord.[3]

"Bless those who persecute you. Bless and do not curse" (Paul says in Romans 12:14, NASB).

We should remember that with Obadiah, as with all the Old Testament books, we are still under the Old Covenant. The culture and Torah considered vengeance against enemies acceptable. The laws of the Torah sealed the deal.

Righteous indignation is always appropriate, in both old and new times. When the prophet chastises the Edomites for "the arrogance of your heart" (Obad. 1:3, NASB), he resembles Jesus rebuking the Pharisees. When he speaks of "the day of the Lord" as drawing near, he echoes the words of Joel and others. Punishment for Edom was also promised at the end of Joel (Joel 3:19).

Christ, the only divine Prophet, also spoke of the end of times in Matthew 24, echoed in Mark 13. Obadiah berating a people who had betrayed their ancestry (connection between Jacob and Esau, from whom Edom descended) is tied also, through the betrayal theme, to Jesus in the garden of Gethsemane, posing the rhetorical question to Judas: "Betrayest thou the Son of Man with a kiss?" (Luke 22:48, KJV).

Once again, Jesus represents the new covenant, with different expectations, outlined clearly in the Sermon on the Mount (reported, for one, in Matthew 5–7). Obadiah expresses the old—where believers could still pray for revenge upon their enemies and God gave to prophets a vision of God's vengeance.

Three-Point Comparison: Obadiah, Revelation, and a Personal Application

Obadiah	Revelation	Application
"All the nations will drink continually and become as if they had never existed." (16b, NASB)	"He also will drink of the wine of the wrath of God [spoken of the followers of the beast]." (14:10a, NASB)	Eventually God's mercy will come to an end. Punishment will then be at hand.
"The arrogance of your heart has deceived you, you who live in the clefts of the rock." (3, NASB)	"For she [Babylon] says in her heart, 'I sit as a queen and I am not a widow, and I will never see mourning.'" (18:7b, NASB)	"…Let him who thinks he stands take heed that he doesn't fall." (1 Cor. 10:13, NASB)
"The deliverers will ascend Mount Zion to judge the mountain of Esau, and the kingdom will be the Lord's (21a, NASB)	"The kingdom of the world has become the kingdom of our Lord and of His Christ; and he will reign forever and ever." (11:15, NASB)	We, God's people, will rejoice in Heaven joining with the choir of Heavenly hosts, singing praises to our Savior and King.

Study Questions

Choose one.

1. Obadiah's book enjoys a distinction among all Old Testament books. What is that distinction? (It's the most recent book/It's the shortest book) _____
   _____

2. What are two possible time periods for the book of Obadiah? (850 and 750 BC or the 840s and 586 BC) __
   _____
   and _____

3. What is the meaning of Obadiah's name? (God is Lord/Servant of the Lord) _____
   _____

4. This book is entirely an invective against what people? (Edom/Amalekites) _____

5. The enemy mentioned was descended from which of God's original family members? (David/Esau)_____
   _____
   _____

How Obadiah Is Still Relevant Today

Verses 8 and 15 warn Israel's enemies about the coming wrath of God on "the day of the Lord." The end of times is on many people's minds. On that day, during the seven-year period of tribulation and then halfway through that period as the world enters into the Great Tribulation when the violence, destruction, and terror are taken to an even higher level, most if not all of God's people will already be in heaven. God will have raptured them there before the punishment begins (if you are a pre-millennial believer).[4]

Some maintain that the 144,000 from twelve tribes represent Jewish people who will turn to God at the end of times, eventually joining the elect and other saints. Dr. David Jeremiah envisions these believers as highly virtu-ous men, all fiercely loyal to their God-given mission to evangelize the world. At the end of times, that is, they will welcome the task of turning as many to Christ as is possible before it is too late. He imagines "144,000 Billy Grahams, bound in faith and sworn, at the risk of their lives, to do Jesus' bidding!" If true, what a day of celebration this will be for all believers![5]

What a day of horror, by way of contrast, for those left behind! Will God's mercy allow an outlet of salvation for the latter? Second Peter 3:9 reminds us that God does not want anyone to perish, which is why there is always the second chance even during the Tribulation. Only after the mark of the beast will there be no chance left for those who take the mark. At that time, God will follow through on His promise of punishment for a particularly vexing enemy. Under the New Covenant, however, we are not to rejoice at the demise of others. We can only pray for our enemies as Jesus has enjoined us to do. If Jesus can pray for the same enemies who nailed him to the cross, we can pray for those who are trying to rob us of spiritual joy.

Obadiah

"Servant of the Lord,"
The OT's shortest book
Contains condemning words
For Edom. Let us look:

Twenty-one verses,
One chapter alone.
Teaming with curses.
Edom undone.

We hear once again
Of Edom's affronts:
In Psalm 137:7—
"Raze it, raze it," their taunts

On Jerusalem's "day"
When Nebuchadnezzar came calling.
David's city was falling.
Edom? Applauding.

Destruction ahead.
Edom is dead
In the water,
The Lord's servant said.

Ruined, betrayed,
Deceived, and afraid.
An ambush is waiting.
A price to be paid.

A hope from the past,
Her cleft in the rocks,
Quite open now
To enemies' attacks.

Negev, Shephelah,
Of Philistine plain;
Ephraim, Samaria,
Benjamin—new names!

Edom's past lands.
Judah, no doubt
will ascend Mount Zion's heights
Judging Edom with a shout.

Notes

1. Unger, 413
2. Ibid.
3. Paul, in Romans 12:19, quotes the first part of Deuteronomy 32:35.
4. Chris Quintana, speaking at the Great Lakes Prophecy Conference, September 7, 2013, on "Modern Israel" at Calvary Chapel, Appleton, Wisconsin has noted that "the Day of the Lord" occurs twenty-five times in the Bible. He adds that the "Day of the Lord" refers to the tribulation period. Pre-tribulation believers do not expect God's people to be present for the tribulation. A merciful Lord will have already safely raptured His people into heaven. The arguments seem to be most compelling for the latter claim.
5. Google: Dr. David Jeremiah on the topic of the 144,000. You will be inspired.

[note to layout: insert photo; centralize]

Jonah—instrument for the most amazing evangelical mass conversion in all of Scripture; an example of God using even an unwilling servant to accomplish His will.

Jonah

ואת־היבשה את־הים אשר־עשה ירא אני השמים אלהי ואת־יהוה
אנוכי עברי אליהם

[He said] to them, "I am a Hebrew, and I
fear the Lord god of Heaven who made
both the sea and the dry land."

—Jonah 1:9 (NASB)

JONAH MEANS "DOVE." The name would be quite fitting
according to today's American slang in the sense that Jonah
preferred to flee and hide rather than face a hated enemy
(even though God did not call him to fight, but rather only
to preach to the Ninevites). We talk about the "hawks" and
the "doves" during wartime, for instance.

He was the son of Amittai, from Gath Hepher, about
three miles northeast of Nazareth. "A short distance to the

north of this site is located the traditional tomb of Jonah in a village called Meshhed."[1]

Jonah shortly preceded Amos under Jeroboam II (782–753 BC). He predicted victory over the Syrians, as recorded in 2 Kings 14:25, and the largest extension of Israel's borders.

Jonah ministered, then, roughly during the time of Amos and Hosea in the north and Isaiah and Micah in the south. Second Kings 14:25 says he announced to Jeroboam II restoration of the ancient boundaries of Israel. Jesus referred to Jonah as factual.

Scholars call the content of the book of Jonah, as literature, predictive typical history. Included in the definition of this type of inspired work would be the book's prophetic motif and its prefiguration of Christ as the sent one.[2]

Details of the latter would include suffering and potential death. First Jonah was in the sea. Then he was in the belly of the fish. Both of these predicaments would have led to death were it not for God's miracle of salvation. Loved ones actually placed the body of Jesus into a tomb. Waves of the sea swamped Jonah. Then he found himself in the belly of the fish. As Jesus ministered to and offered salvation even to Gentiles, so did Jonah minister to them, offering them deliverance and salvation. See passages like Matthew 12:38–48: "The Sign of Jonah" passage, and Luke 11:29–32 (same topic, different occasion, slightly different context).

Some have doubted that a man could be swallowed by a large fish then live to tell about it. Believers, looking for extra biblical proof, sometimes point to the story of James Bartley, the nineteenth century Irish whaler, to show that it not only could but has happened in more recent times. Others say the latter story was not true at all and offer arguments against it. Believers know, however, that with or without a James Bartley account, God's Word needs no scaffolding to merit our belief. God said it through His prophet; Jesus the Son of God validated it, and we know that for the Master of the Universe, such a feat is mere child's play. What about the theme of God wanting to save even non-Hebrews?

In the accounts of Elijah and Elisha, as told in 1 and 2 Kings, God calls His prophet to evangelize heathen peoples. Elijah, for example, ministers to the widow from Zarephath. Elisha reaches out to Naaman, the Syrian military official, and heals his leprosy. In addition, the book of Jonah gives an unmistakable message that God is a God of both Hebrew and non-Hebrew. As such, the Word reminds us that God would love to save all of mankind (1 Tim. 2:4). We need to witness to even our enemies—those who seem farthest away from God and His Word. Nineveh was the enemy of Jonah and of God's people.

Nineveh was also the greatest city of its day. Yet Nahum (probably written between 663 and 612 BC, predicted its fall.[3]

The proud and wicked city did, in fact, fall in 612 BC under Nebuchadnezzar, king of the Babylonians. We must ask ourselves, Is God sending us signals of warning that punishment is in store for our nation? Will states voting to allow gay marriage and a president who promotes public funding of abortion and the gay lifestyle push the United States over the edge of a jealous God's tolerance level? Note that the ministry of Jonah was threefold really:

1) It first occurred among God's people as reported in 2 Kings 14:25.
2) It then occurred on the boat with the pagan polytheistic sailors traveling from Joppa to Tarshish.
3) It concluded (at least as far as we know) in the city of Nineveh, chief city (at the time, not yet the capital) of the Assyrians—future tool of punishment of the northern kingdom of Israel.

In the first phase of his ministry, he apparently performed well as the Sovereign Lord (who sees and knows all) and thought Jonah worthy of his ultimate evangelism ministry. In the mezzanine and brief second portion, he performs like a coward, ending by offering to commit suicide, apparently believing God was ready to kill him anyway as punishment for fleeing. In the final portion, he begins in repentance, performs his God-assigned task, but then regrets he did something that will result in possible spiritual salvation for the hated Assyrians. In a sense, here, he is much like the seed planted on rocky soil; he flourishes for moments but then withers as time goes on. Sometimes God also works through us despite our sinful selves.

Curiously, from Assyrian records, there was a turn to monotheism around the time of Jonah. A sovereign God may have orchestrated two plagues and a total eclipse around the same time to prepare the hearts of Israel's nemesis.[4]

The account of Jonah teaches us many things, among the most important of which are no mere man may thwart the plans of the sovereign Lord, Master of the universe. God will use man, nature, as well as creatures of the land or sea, to accomplish his purposes. Finally, when the Lord comes calling with a plan for our lives, the best thing, the only thing really, we can do is bend our will to his and rejoice in the privilege of the Lord using us to bring about his purpose.

Jonah was a type of Christ when he lay down and slept in the hold of a ship during stormy weather. When he sacrificed himself to save others, he also typified Christ, in a sense. He even grew up in a town called Amittai, not far from Nazareth where the Savior became a man.

Yet the similarity stops where it comes to complete obedience and submission to God. Jesus was always humbly and willingly at the disposal his divine Father. May we learn from the story of Jonah not the consequences of disobedience but the blessings that come from surrender to God and Jesus Christ.

Other Points of Interest in Jonah

Jonah, at the beginning of chapter 4, is bemoaning the saving of souls in Nineveh. This account bears some resemblance to a scene from Shakespeare's *Hamlet*. In the play, his stepfather has secretly and treacherously killed Hamlet's (namesake) biological father, the original king, and married Hamlet's mother. The mother is oblivious to the murder. Hamlet comes to have his suspicions confirmed through a dream and, seeking vengeance, begins plotting the death of the wicked usurper king, Claudius, his uncle and now his stepfather. At one point in the play, Hamlet has a monologue. The playwright brings the audience into the thought stream of a deeply troubled young prince. The king is in prayer in the palace chapel. Hamlet, from his place of hiding, watching the king pray, contemplates doing the deed at that precise time. He decides to wait, however, for a more opportune moment when he will more likely not only kill the body but also be the divine agent in sending the soul of his nemesis to hell. This puts a human twist on the biblical tenet of a God who is able to destroy both body and soul in hell. Hamlet wants to catch the king in sin and then kill him. God's justice will do the rest. Hamlet's hateful state of mind resembles that of Jonah in chapter 4, except that Jonah will have no chance to harm his perceived enemies. The latter is what so depresses him (where depression, as the experts say, often results from powerlessness manifested as anger turned outside in.)

Read Nahum 3 for insight on Assyria's and Nineveh's sins that eventually led to their destruction. The city reverted to their old ways, after the repentant generation of Jonah's day. What about Jonah's problematic attitude, again, though?

Jesus told a parable about different kinds of seed (Matt. 13:3–9): one falls among the rocks (verse 5) and blooms for a while then withers. Jonah also blooms for a while (early ministry mentioned at 2 Kings 14:25) then withers (his attempted escape to Tarshish), then blooms (in a penitent completion of his evangelistic trip to Nineveh), then withers again (by way of his regret that God would have mercy on this people who had been the source of so much misery for God's people).

In the second withering phase of his spiritual journey, Jonah sat down east of the city with a sun from the east that beat down upon him. Some believe that the east, interestingly, is often the direction away from God. God placed a cherubim and flaming sword at the east end of the garden to bar entrance. Cain went east after God's unsuccessful evangelistic effort upon his heart. God banished Ishmael and Hagar to the east for the last time when Sarah had had enough. Israelites had to approach God from the east side of the tabernacle, each progression toward God being away from that same direction. Even in the New Testament, wise men came from the east, headed west as they approached the promised Messiah of Israel.[5]

The little epilogue at the end with the flourishing, then withering plant, seems like a bit of poetic justice from God's point of view. The plight of the plant seems symbolic to Jonah's history with God, during his calling to minister at Nineveh.

Finally, Matthew 12:38–40 and Luke 11:29–32 both mention the "sign of Jonah" response that Jesus gave to the hateful Pharisees and "teachers of the law."

Passages and Ideas Bearing on Jonah

Jonah went to Joppa. Some have pointed out Joppa as being the only harbor between Mt. Carmel and Egypt at the time.[6]

From there, he wanted to sail to Tarshish, probably in Spain, near Gibraltar.[7]

Nineveh and Tarshish represent opposite ends of the Mediterranean Levantine commercial sphere.[8]

"The word of the Lord came" also appears in Elijah (1 Kings 17:8), Jeremiah, Hosea, Joel, Haggai, and Zechariah.

As mentioned, in some ways Jonah is a type of Christ, he sleeps on board the ship during a storm. He ministers to the gentiles (both on the ship—not so successfully, and, later, with great success, in the city of Nineveh). Jesus would minister to the Samaritan woman at the well.

The comparison crumbles, however, when God calms the storm through Jonah's offer to commit suicide by getting himself thrown into the sea. Contrast this with Jesus, Son of God, who calmed the storm through his sovereignty as the all-powerful Son of God.

In Matthew 7:24–26, Jesus's parable comparing faith built upon a rock and faith built upon sand, remarkably contains a visual parallel between the storm, waves, wind, and rain at the beginning of the Jonah account. Jonah's faith, as discovered from his disobedient flight, mirrors a dwindling faith that has him headed toward destruction—both physical and spiritual. The former danger resulted from the latter malaise or lapse. This is especially tragic in view of his position as God's chosen mouthpiece of the moment.

In Psalm 139:7–12, David wrote, "Where can I go to flee from the Lord?" hundreds of years before Jonah lived and wrote, yet these words seem to describe Jonah's situation quite well. Maybe the Lord gave David a bit of the prophetic gift, applicable most fittingly for Jonah's response to God's post-flight discipline for the wayward prophet. Certainly, Jonah, as a chosen prophet of the Lord, would have been familiar with the Psalms. One thing is certain: our helplessness before God is part of the universal principle of our full dependence upon him.

As an aside and just for information's sake, casting lots was a common way to determine guilt at the time Jonah wrote his book.[9]

God spared a penitent Nineveh just like He postponed the ruin of Ahab and his family when Ahab repented in sackcloth and ashes. God loves a repentant heart and would do anything to save the penitent, even those who are farthest from his heart and ways.

God working a conversion of pagans through his prophet is a theme we have seen before: here a city of over two hundred thousand follows the lead of their king. In the story of Elijah, it was the woman from Zarephath. In the case of Elisha, it was the Shunammite woman and Nahaman the Syrian. People often say that the Old Testament is the New Testament concealed. The New Testament, on the other hand, is the Old Testament revealed.[10]

Paul would one day write that God had revealed to him (Paul) a great spiritual secret. God's people were to share with Gentiles the Gospel good news of salvation through faith in Jesus Christ. Again, the Old Testament had been hinting at it all along.

It is difficult to try and use Jonah as a role model as we have been able to do with most of the other prophets. However, sometimes we learn best by looking at how NOT to do things. Jonah reminds us that all too often we run when God comes calling. We want what is convenient, warm, and fuzzy if possible, well inside our comfort zone, within the status quo ante.

On the flip side, if God can take a reluctant prophet and use him to accomplish easily the most amazing miracle of mass conversion in all of Bible history, again—against his will—think what he could accomplish with us if we were willing to step outside the box, in surrender to him. Once again, God will be using Jonah to accomplish his purpose, in spite of himself. For that, we can be grateful to "the dove."

Three-Point Comparison: Jonah, Revelation, and a Personal Application

Jonah	Revelation	Application
Jonah 1:1–3 (The call of Jonah.	Revelation 4:1–2 (The call of John.)	What will YOU do when God calls?
Jonah 3:3–4 (preaching at Nineveh). invitation to seek God, judgment, and a warning.	Revelation 14:6–11: Three angels preach:	The "fear of the Lord is the beginning of wisdom."
Jonah 2:3: Jonah is cast into the deep.	Revelation 20:10: Devil's abyss.	Falls into trouble may be God's way of saving us, but only if we pay heed.

Study Questions

Choose one.

1. What does the name of Jonah mean? (Eagle/Dove)
   _____

2. What was the name of Jonah's father? (Buzi/Amittai)
   _____

3. Where was Jonah from? (Nazareth/Gath Hepher)
   _____

4. What prophet came just after Jonah? (Amos/Jeremiah)
   _____ What time period? (850–800
   BC / 782–753 BC) _____

5. What two amazing events occurred in connection with
   Jonah? (He was eaten by a whale and rematerialized/
   He was swallowed by a very large fish and regurgitated)

   _____

   and (he joyfully/grudgingly) _____ evange-
   lized the entire city of Nineveh.

The Relevance of Jonah Yet Today

One day God will hold all of us accountable for the lives that we have chosen to live. Do we choose to live lives dedicated to the Lord, or are we, rather, servants of the flesh? How did we react when the Lord came calling, challenging us to show signs of the fruits of faith? Did we run away from our responsibilities to the Bridegroom? Have we now repented and finally, like prodigals, returned to our service? On what occasions have we finally allowed God to use us but then developed an attitude of resentment toward the one who loved us so much he sent his son to die for us and the son willingly did take our place? Can we also try that one again? The Lord loves a cheerful giver—both those who give of their time as well as those who give their tithes and offerings. Can we serve in joy, in an act of progressive sanctification, and remove the Old Man past pattern of one step forward and two steps back?

Jonah

Jonah, the "Dove,"
Hailed from Gath Hepher,
Three miles northeast of
The Lord's Nazareth.

When did he serve?
Just before Amos,
Under Jeroboam II,
This prophet- famous.

He wasn't being true
To his calling.
"To Nineveh you'll go,"
But Jonah proved slow.

"Down" is a theme
Fitting for him:
Check Rasnake and Barber.
Their book you can skim:[11]

Down in spirits,
Down thoroughly,
Down to Joppa,
Down by the sea;

From there down to Tarshish
(Quite probably Spain).
Down into the ship
Where he lay "down" again.

Down into the sea
They tossed him overboard.
Down into the fish, surely,
He slid; wait, there's more!

God's fish gave Jonah a one-way trip
To Nineveh. This time he would not slip.
Encouraged now, by divine restoration—
An anointed message for an enemy nation:

"Forty days, Nineveh,
Till you're overthrown,"
Forty days until Yahweh
Throws them down.

What happened next
Is in the text,
After Obadiah,
Preceding Micah:

Chapter four: verse eleven,
Information from heaven:
An entire city in sackcloth and ashes,
Conversion for the ages.

Jonah's response?
To his shame—remorse.
Apparently, he thought God's threat real,
Meant to result in their death. No joy could he feel

With Nineveh forgiven.
Outside the city, to the east he sat down
Under shade of a tree—driven,
And wearing a frown.

Prophet and Lord
Engage in discourse:
"Death is better;
What could be worse?"[12]

Said "the dove"
To the one above.
A plant first for shade,
Then taken away,

Resembling Jonah:
Who, obeying God's command,
Then taking a stand—
This time in spirit he ran.

One lesson for all:
When receiving God's call,
Each mission—embrace;
For blessings, give thanks.

Notes

1. Unger, 415
2. Website: "Desiring God Ministry, Bible Talk under 'Jonah.'"
3. NIV Study Bible, 1373
4. Unger, 417
5. *Life Principles from the Prophets of the Old Testament.*
6. Nelson, 332
7. Ibid., 600
8. *Life Principles from the Prophets of the Old Testament*, 57
9. NASB Study Bible, 1295, which also goes on to say, "The casting of lots was a custom widely practiced in the ancient near East."
10. The quote is from St. Augustine, fifth century AD.
11. Barber and Rasnake, *Life Principles from the Prophets the Old Testament.*
12. Jonah 4:8

[note to layout: insert photo; centralize]

God's surprise for the world: The Messiah would come from the little town of Bethlehem in Judea, as foretold by Micah.

Micah

ואתה   לחיות צעיר אפרתה בית־לחם   יהוה באלפי

יצא לי ממך יהוה באלפי עולם מימי מקדם ומוצאתיו בישראל מושל לחיות

> But as for you, Bethlehem Ephrata, too little to
> be among the clans of Judah, from you one will
> go forth for me to be ruler in Israel. his goings
> forth are from long ago, from the days of eternity.

—Micah 5:2 (NASB)

HIS NAME MEANS "who is like the Lord?" He was from the town of Moresheth Gath (Mic. 1:1, 14), in southern Judah. Images from country life abound in Micah. He was a contemporary of Isaiah and Hosea. Speaking out strongly against false prophets who gave false hopes to the people, he himself tells us (Mic. 1:1) that he served during the reigns of three kings from Judah: Jotham, Ahaz, and Hezekiah. He must have served, therefore, between 750 and 687 BC.[1]

Some have drawn a comparison between Micah and Isaiah: Isaiah being a "court poet, statesman, and voice to kings" who "addressed himself to political questions." Micah, on the other hand, was "a rustic, evangelist, social reformer, and herald to the common people who treated mainly personal religion and social morality."[2]

In Micah 1:6, we see the destruction of Samaria predicted. This happened in 722–721 BC. The social conditions referred to would have predated the religious reforms under Hezekiah (715–686). Another way people say Micah and Isaiah have similarities is their style of writing. The style of Micah, some say, is similar to that of Isaiah (vigorous with many figures of speech).[3]

The opening verses of Micah predict destruction for Samaria (the capital, representing the northern kingdom) and Jerusalem (the capital of Judah and the southern kingdom). The destruction is described in terms of similes like "melting mountains, splitting apart valleys, water rushing down a slope, [being turned into] a heap of rubble."

Micah's prediction in 5:2 that a king would be born from lowly Bethlehem has ramifications on two levels: The "ruler in Israel" spoken of (in 5:2) was Christ—Prophet, Priest, (and most relevant to the context) King. During Jesus's ministry, at the Sermon on the Mount, the Lord and Messiah preached: "Blessed are the meek for they shall inherit the earth" (Matt. 5:5). Jesus himself who meekly accepted his fate from Pilate and others during the Passion Week, will return triumphant at the end of times and lay claim on the world, reigning supreme for one thousand years. In Micah 5:2 the prophet dwells more on the first advent. Chapter 4 on the other hand, refers to the end of times.

Comparisons between Words and Scenes of Micah and Those of Other Prophets

Micah	Other Prophets
The wages of prostitutes (Mic. 1:7).	Hosea's marriage to Gomer, a prostitute, and God using this as a symbol for the sins of the people especially worshiping of the Asherahs and Baals.
Rhetorical questions (Mic. 1:5):	Can a woman forget her nursing child? (Isa. 49:15a, NASB)
What is Jacob's transgression? Is it not Samaria? What is Judah's high place?	Cannot my hand redeem? (Isa. 50:2) Who will contend with me? (Isa. 50:8, NASB)

Micah	Other Prophets
Is it not Jerusalem?	Who will condemn me? (Isa. 50:9, NIV) Where is the fury of the oppressor? (Isa. 51:13b, NASB)
God will destroy Samaria and the northern kingdom: "I will make Samaria a heap." (Mic. 1:6, NASB)	"Name her (the second daughter) 'Lo-ru-ha-ma' for I will no more have compassion upon the house of Israel." (Hosea 1:6, NASB)
I will surely assemble all of you. (Jacob Mic. 2:12, NASB)	"Unless the Lord Godof Israel had left us a few survivors" (Isa. 1:9)

Themes in Micah	Passage
A return to the days of Moses and God's wonders in Egypt and the wilderness	"According to the days of thy coming out of the land of Egypt will I show unto him marvelous things." (Mic. 7:15)
God will provide for a remnant of His people no matter what else happens: "I will make the lame a remnant."	Micah 2:12, 4:7, 5:7

Themes in Micah	Passage
God will punish Israel's enemies.	Micah 4:12–13 Arise and Thresh, O Daughter of Zion!
Specifically, God will punish Assyria.	"And they shall waste the land ofAssyria." (Mic. 5:6)
God will punish both Israel in the north in the south.	"What is the transgression and Judah of Jacob?Is it not Samaria? What are the highplaces of Judah? Are they not Jerusalem?" (Mic. 1:5)
The Messiah shall come out of the small town of Bethlehem, in the outlying part called Ephrata.	Micah 5:2
God does not want vain sacrifices and wicked behavior in every other facet of our life; he wants the real deal: that we act justly and live a godly life. New Testament Christians attempt to lead a life patterned after Christ.	Micah 6:7–8

Themes in Micah	Passage
People are listening to whatever prophet tells them what they want to hear (false prophets doing this, that is), not what God intended for His people to hear and know.	"If a man walking in the spirit and falsehood do lie, saying, 'I will prophesy unto thee of wine and of strong drink. He shall even be the the prophet of this people.'" (Mic. 2:11, KJV)

Other Ideas in Micah

We all like stories with happy endings. It would be nice to have a prophet start out praising people for the good they are doing. That would be encouraging and refreshing. Even John, in his letters to the seven churches (in the book of Revelation) had two churches that were doing Christianity right: Smyrna (the "persecuted church" as many have called it) and Philadelphia (the "virtuous church," again some have called it). Such places in this world are the exception, however. The reality is, if everyone had been doing what was right to begin with, God may not have needed to send messengers. The prophets were there to praise and encourage them when they did right, true. Yet I think we must agree, for the most part, God sent prophets because God's children had gone astray and needed correction. The first address to the people from Micah informs them that God is "against you" (Mic. 1:2).

Haggai opened up also by informing the recently returned remnant of Judah that he had been against them, and they didn't even know it: "'You look for much but behold, it comes to little; when you bring it home, I blow it away. Why?' declares the Lord of hosts, 'Because of my house which lies desolate, while each of you runs to his own house'" (Hag. 1:9, NASB). On what blessings is your church, your state, your country missing out due to neglecting the Lord's house? What can we do to get back into the Lord's good favor? This is not rocket science—worship the Lord. Obey God's commands. Live for Jesus and others!

Although the opening is addressed to "O peoples, all of you, O earth and all who are in it," he means most specifically the people of Judah and Israel, the southern and northern kingdom. In 1:1–7, we hear of the punishment that is in store for those living as pagans in rebellion against God. Micah 1:8–11 shows Micah mourning for the people, soon to be under attack, under the wrath of God. He will go barefoot (a sign of mourning) and walk naked in the streets (possibly, instead, in a loincloth) to show his mourning and sadness.[4]

Comparison: Micah, Revelation, and a Personal Application

Micah	Revelation	Application
"But thou, Bethlehem Ephphrata, though thou be little among the clans of Judah, yet out of thee shall he come... that is to be ruler over all Israel." (Mic. 5:2, KJV)	"Worthy is the lamb that was slain to receive power and riches and wisdom and might and honor..." (Rev. 5:12b, NASB)	The King of Kings is robed in humility as an example for us, His people, to follow. Jesus promised that the gentle or the meek would "inherit the earth" (Matt. 5:5).
"They shall beat their swords into plowshares and their spears into pruning hooks." (Mic. 4:3, KJV)	"And he will wipe away every tear from their eyes; and there will no longer be any death." (Rev. 21:4a, NASB)	Heaven, the final destination on the Christian journey will be a place of complete peace.

Micah	Revelation	Application
"He has told you, O man what is good; and what does the Lord require of you, but to do justice and to love kindness, and to walk humbly with your God. (Mic. 6:8, NASB)	"I know thy works [Church at Philadelpia] Behold I have set before thee an open door which no man can shut. For thou hast a a little strength, and hast kept my word. (Rev. 3:8, KJV)	"Eye hath not seen nor ear heard, neither have entered into the heart of man what God hath prepared for those who love him. (1 Cor. 2:9, KJV)
"The good man is perished out of the earth, and there is none upright among men: they all lie in wait for blood; they hunt every man his brother with a net." (Micah 7:2, KJV)	"And the rest of the men which were not killed by these plagues yet repented not of the works of their hands, that they should not worship devils… neither repented they of their murders." (Rev. 9:20–21)	What will a just God do with a mighty nation, a blessed nation, that continues to sanction abortion on demand and homosexuality?

Apocalyptic Passages

"It shall come to pass in the latter days that the mountain of the house of the Lord shall be established as the highest of the mountains." (Mic. 4:1–7, ESV)

"For, behold, the Lord cometh forth from his place. He will come down, and tread upon the high places of the earth. The mountains will melt under him." (Mic. 1:3–4a, NASB)

Memorable Passages

"If a man walking after wind and falsehood had told lies and said, 'I will speak out to you concerning wine and liquor,' he would be spokesman to this people. (Mic. 2:11, NASB)

"But thou, Bethlehem Ephrata, though thou be little among the clans of Judah, yet out of thee shall one come who shall be ruler in Israel, whose goings forth have been from of old, from everlasting." (Mic. 5:2, KJV)

"They shall beat their sword into plowshares, and their spears into pruning hooks: nation shall not lift up a sword against nation; neither shall they learn war any more." (Mic. 4:3b, KJV)

Micah Review Questions

Choose one.

Answer these questions:

1. The capital of Israel, the northern kingdom, was (Jerusalem/Samaria). _____
2. The capital of Judah, the Southern Kingdom, was (Jerusalem/Bethel)._____
3. Out of these three kings, who was the best (in God's eyes): Jotham, Ahaz, and Hezekiah? (Circle one)
4. Who was the worst of the three kings during Micah's ministry? _____
5. Someone has said Judah was guilty of "sanctimonious orthodoxy." In your own words, what do you think that means? (Ostentatious formal worship, lacking in real substance/ pious observance during worship of false gods) _____
   _____
6. One of the three kings during Micah's reign did well in every way but one. What one thing did he fail to do? (Throw away household idols/do away with idols in high places) _____
   _____

7. What enemy defeated the northern kingdom and carried them into captivity? (Babylon/Assyria) _____
    _____

8. Who defeated the southern kingdom (over one hundred years later) and carried them away? (Persia/Babylon) _____

9. Did the North ever return? (No/Yes) _____
    _____

10. Did the South ever return? (Yes/No)_____

The Relevance of Micah for Us

What modern spokesman for the Lord, known for eloquence, do we have who has come out of a rural setting to speak to the common man in ways he can relate to? Billy Graham to a certain extent? Micah's message about the Lord looking for true worshippers who love him, not experts on externals who have little heart for others, is a timeless reminder for believers of all times: "Man looks at the outward appearance, but the Lord looks at the heart" (1 Sam. 16:7b, NASB). Samuel told Jesse when the latter questioned the choice of David, the youngest and most unpretentious of all his many sons, to be king of God's people and royal ancestor of the Messiah. Churches that focus too much on formalism and not enough on the law and gospel of the Scriptures can fall into the trap of which Micah warns.

The message that a Savior would come from an unpretentious place ("Though you be small among the clans of Judah") should be no surprise to those who know Jesus as the Champion of humility, the One who, in the Sermon on the Mount (as related in Matthew 5–7), promised that "the meek shall inherit the earth" (Matt. 5:5).

James echoed this sentiment in chapter one when he asked the rhetorical question: Listen, my beloved brethren: did not God choose the poor of this world to be rich in faith and heirs of the kingdom which He promised to those who love Him? (James 5:2, NASB). We can see the words of both Jesus, our Savior, and James as having men of faith such as Micah in mind.

Micah

Bethlehem Ephrata…
"Oh little town…" in song
In Micah 5:2
"The least" becomes strong.

"The meek shall inherit
The earth," Jesus said:[5]
This small town would merit
The birth of our Lord.

Micah, Isaiah: striking contrast.
The former a rustic.
The latter consulted
Kings in their palace.

Like all other prophets,
He held nothing back.
The north, Micah says,
Will fall under attack.

Which, in 722 BC, it did.
"Melting mountains," trouble,
"Splitting valleys, waters slip,
Samaria, a rubble."

Ekah? [How?] Samaria—[6]
(Central place of) Jacob's sins."
That of Judah?
Jerusalem!"

Capital cities of north and south,
Seeds of corruption.
Yet, the meek who inherit the earth,
God's remnant, are not done.

Micah goes barefoot,
A sign of mourning,
At destruction afoot.
His sadness? A warning.

Yet, after all,
Swords become plowshares
When good men heed the call.
God's reward? All free of cares.

Then again, the people are wicked,
The prophet nonplussed.
"Nothing is good left to eat," he said.
God's bride? A bust!

In chapter seven,
Last one in the book,
"Who is like the Lord?"[7]
Gives heaven a look.

Then, like Habakkuk 2:1:
"I will watch for the Lord…"
In the end, we have won:
"Who like God?" has heard

And seen the coming Messiah.
The end of the world—
At the end of the seventh and last chapter:
Wicked are under dread, righteous confirmed.

Notes

1. *Nelson's Compact Bible Dictionary*, 404
2. *Unger's Bible Handbook*, 418
3. NIV Study Bible, 1363–4
4. Ibid., 1365
5. Matthew 5:5, spoken at the beginning of the Sermon on the Mount as recorded in Matthew 5–7
6. *Ekah*, not in this text, but the author's recognition of the forlorn tone, recalling the Hebrew title, *Ekah?*, "Why?" of Lamentations.
7. "Who is like the Lord?" is the meaning of Micah's name

[note to layout: insert photo; centralize]

Nahum represents the idea that the wicked's demise will be complete. Like Israel fell to Assyria so Nineveh, capital city of a doomed ungodly civilization, will itself disappear.

Nahum

שלום משמיע מבשר רגלי על־ההרים הנה

Behold on the mountains the feet of
him who brings good news!

—Nahum 1:15 (NASB)

THE NAME NAHUM means "comforter" or "consoler." The
words of Nahum 2:1 seem to show the prophet living up
to his name—providing uplifting and inspirational words
to all who would hear. He came from a city named Elkosh.
We do not know the exact location of Elkosh. The address
to Judah, however, in 1:15 makes it likely Nahum was from
Judah.[1] His prophecy concerns the future demise of the
Assyrian empire and its capital, Nineveh. Descriptions of
Assyrian power make it likely that Nahum's ministry was
between 661 and 612 BC (the fall of Assyria).[2] This dating

puts him, like the Judean prophets Jeremiah and Ezekiel, during the reign of the wonderful and godly Josiah. While God called Jonah to extend to Nineveh a warning resulting in a stunning spiritual victory of religious conversion, Nahum brings the history of this hated nation back full circle to its original expectation. Death by the sword comes to those who would choose to live by the sword (Jesus's words to Peter in Matthew 26:52, a rephrasing, in turn, of Genesis 9:6. The latter is part of God's post-flood covenant with Noah). Assyria, as God's pawn, had dealt a deathblow to the northern ten tribes. Now God would work through the power (Babylon) to punish the remnant southern two tribes. Those looking in from the outside on the Christian experience might find it ironic that the prophet whose name means "consoler" would be preaching primarily a message of destruction toward a hated enemy. Nahum's focus on revenge brings to mind the words and pathos of Psalm 137: "By the rivers of Babylon." The latter portrays the pain of God's people during the Babylonian captivity when the captors cruelly demanded a song of mirth from their recently captured slaves. Little did the Babylonians know that the singers, in their unknown tongue of Hebrew, were rejoicing at the thought that one day someone would recompense Babylon in like manner for what they had done to others. Dashing their babies on the rocks (as they had done to God's people) was the final thought and word picture of this psalm. Nahum, "the consoler," consoles his people with a vision of destruction for, in this case, the Assyrians. Vengeance as an acceptable sentiment for God's people is a facet of the Old Testament Covenant. The love, forgiveness, and turn-the-other-cheek sentiment of the New Testament Covenant, by way of contrast, are hallmarks of Christ's new relationship with His church.

On a final and different note, John, God's primary New Testament chosen messenger for the end of times, would be privileged with the vision of a triumphant Christ, returning to gather up His people and remove them to a place of safety (the rapture). The rapture would serve as a prelude to His coming back again, leading an army of angels. The latter would result in the final transference to the lake of fire for all enemies of the truth, of Jesus Christ, and of God's people. In a sense, then, Nahum's message is a dress rehearsal for John's message in Revelation. The overthrowing of Nineveh, a long despised enemy, is equally a dress rehearsal for the final defeat of the enemy of God and man since the days of Adam and Eve in the Garden—Satan.

Observations on Nahum

When the prophet says (in chapter 1:3, NASB), "In whirlwind and storm is his way," he evokes a word image of Ezekiel 1:4 (NASB): "As I looked, behold, a storm wind was coming from the north." Further on in chapter 1 (verse 5, NASB), he notes how "mountains quake because of him and the hills dissolve." The latter evokes memory of Psalm 46:3b (NASB): "Though the mountains quake at its (that of the sea) swelling pride." The psalmist wrote all of Psalm 46, in fact, as a demonstration of the majesty and sovereignty of God over all His creation. Thankfully, he's on our side: "God is our refuge and strength," the psalmist begins. A variation on that theme also marks the end of this beautiful psalm. We can find Nahum's version of God as the protector in verse 7: "The Lord is good, a stronghold in the day of trouble" (NASB). What do the similarities tell us? The Lord has informed Nahum through the psalms. Here is evidence, then, of the exegetical principle, that the Bible interprets itself. To be more precise, in this case, the Word informs itself: Scripture, that is, finds deeper meaning by drawing upon itself to relate similar ideas in a different context and time.

Nahum 1:15 (NASB) offers another example: "Behold, on the mountains the feet of him who brings good news." This is a simplification of Isaiah's earlier but further developed, "How beautiful upon the mountains are the feet of him who brings good news" (Isa. 52:7, NASB). Since Isaiah precedes Nahum, in some estimates, by the better part of a century, Nahum would have borrowed from Isaiah, just as he appears to have borrowed from Psalms. The similarity between Ezekiel and Nahum, however, may be more coincidental than the idea of Ezekiel (who came later) borrowing from Nahum. Ezekiel actually experienced the vision of God approaching in the form of a whirlwind. Nahum mentions this more matter of factly as an attribute of God that the Lord has revealed to him.

In Acts 2, finally, when the wind came bursting into the room on Pentecost to inaugurate the New Testament church, anyone who was aware of the appropriate Ezekiel and Nahum passages may have felt God, in this manifestation as the Holy Spirit, was once again living up to his billing.

Comparison: Nahum, Revelation, and a Personal Application

Nahum	Revelation	Application
A jealous and avenging God is the Lord (1:2).	"Faithful and True, and he… wages war; his eyes are a flame of fire" (19:11–12).	To fight our three deadly foes (the devil, the world, and our sinful flesh), we have the Lord on our side.
"Mountains quake because of Him" (1:5, NASB).	"Every mountain and island were moved out of their places" (6:14 b, NASB)	Elijah felt the mountain quake also during his cave experience with the Lord. Yet it was a whisper that he heard, when God began to communicate with him personally.
"His wrath is poured out like fire" (1:6 b, NASB).	"Then the angel took the censer and filled it with the fire of the altar, and threw it to the earth" (8:5a, NASB).	The Lord plays with fire while we look to obey.

Study Questions

Choose one.

1. What is the meaning of Nahum's name? (Dove or pigeon/Comforter or consoler) _____ or _____ _____.

2. What city did Nahum come from? (Bethel/Elkosh) _____

3. What was the general location of Nahum's hometown, probably? (Benjamin/Judah) _____ _____

4. What is the main topic of Nahum's message from the Lord? (God will punish Babylon /God will punish Nineveh) _____

5. What is the probable time for Nahum? (Between 661 and 612 BC/ Between 490 and 460 BC) _____ _____

Why Nahum Still Matters to Us Today

Like Nahum's name ("comforter" or "consoler"), Christians today can take heart in his message. We are in the world, but we are not of the world. We hear this often. Jesus tells us in the Sermon on the Mount (Matt. 5:13–16) that we are to be salt and light in the world; salt because life without Christ is bland and going nowhere. We should be like light, because the world seems to love stumbling in the darkness. Jesus has told us not to delight in the ruin of the wicked. Instead, when we see them falling and know it's from the Lord, we are to take greater stock in the Great Commission—to get the word out to all men, for the Lord would have all men to be saved.[3] Paul's variation on the theme of being salt and light in the world was to "become all things" (within reason, and still according to the principle of righteousness) to all men so that more might be saved (1 Tim. 2:4). May we also be that light, not the one set under a basket (as so many of us are tempted to be, sometimes out of spite for a world immersed in ungodly living), but rather the one that "lights up the whole room so that all can benefit from it."[4]

Nahum

Nahum, the "Comforter"
From Judah's Elkosh
Reveals the future.
Nineveh is lost.

The "Consoler" probably
From Josiah's day:
Seventh century BC
Latter half of it, okay?

In Nahum a poet has found his home
Quite fitting that here, then, he has earned his stay.[5]
Metaphor and simile, rhetorical questions abound—[6]
Nineveh is a lion. All others her prey.

Jonah's mission,
A grudging success:
As Nineveh with passion,
To God's calling said "yes."

Nahum, now later, tells them "You're dead."
Who can endure the wrath of God?
Your devices are useless.
Man the fortress, watch the road.[7]

Chariots race madly[8]
Those terrors of old,
Prepared now quite badly
With their end foretold.

This is a scene
OT believers cherish:
Their enemies, no dream,
Defeated. They perish!

Notes

1. ESV Study Bible, 1709
2. Unger, 423: between the conquest of No-Amon (Thebes) in Egypt and Nineveh's fall in 612 BC.
3. 1 Tim. 2:4, reworked and rephrased in 2 Peter 3:9
4. Matthew 5:15–16 paraphrased
5. "Here," meaning in this poem
6. You can find the references to poetic tropes in the NASB, page 1308 under the section heading—"Literary Style."
7. Nahum 2:2
8. Ibid., 2:4

[note to layout: insert photo; centralize]

Habakkuk, a prophet who dialogued with God in the spirit of Moses and Abraham, taking advantage of the Lord's golden teaching moment, and humbly accepting God's judgment—an example for us all.

Habakkuk

תשמע ולא שועתי יהוה עד־אנה

How long, O Lord, will I cry for
help, and You will not hear?

—Habakkuk 1:2a (NASB)

HIS NAME MEANS "embrace" or "wrestle." All sources say
that little is known about Habakkuk, "except that he was a
contemporary of Jeremiah and a man of vigorous faith…"[1]
Since he was a contemporary of Jeremiah, this puts him at
the end of good king Josiah (640–609 BC) and at the beginning of wicked Jehoiakim (609–598). Habakkuk would
have been familiar with the death of Josiah, his beloved
and godly king, in the Valley of Megiddo in 609 BC when
the latter fell at the hands of Pharaoh Necho.[2]

Four years later, Nebuchadnezzar defeated Necho at the Battle of Carchemish. Many put Habakkuk's book around the Battle of Carchemish (605).[3]

In a discussion between God and his prophet, the Mighty One promised destruction first for Judah (for their unrepentant wickedness), then for Babylon, the oppressor (for their arrogance, incorrigible cruelty, and barbaric excesses). Habakkuk probably saw an early fulfillment of his prophecy of destruction in 597 when Babylon attacked Jerusalem.[4] The prophecy occurs in the form of a dialogue between the prophet and God. Other prophets who employed this literary technique (including dialogue between prophet and representative of God) were Samuel (briefly as a boy in the temple), Elijah, Jonah, Hosea, Isaiah, Jeremiah, Ezekiel, and Daniel (in chapter 9, involving a visit from the angel Gabriel). Back to the king, what a great example and breath of fresh air King Josiah must have been for those who served under him! Coming to the throne at the young age of eight, by the time he was sixteen, he had made a public commitment that he was going to serve the Lord.[5]

Josiah's purity of heart recalls Joshua who said, "But as for me and my house, we will serve the Lord" (Josh. 24:15b, NASB) Josiah's decision to return to the Lord, moreover, had a precedent—Hezekiah's reforms during his reign (from 728 BC to 686 BC). The fact that both were kings (who could do whatever they wanted and who were preceded by a long string of evil kings) made their pious allegiance to the one true God all the more impressive. Habakkuk, Jeremiah, and the others who witnessed and experienced Josiah's welcome devotion and respect for his God must have loved this king. Judah finally had a king who gave them a righteous backdrop for a message! The prophet's message this time was one with teeth—a call to righteousness with the backing of their most powerful citizen! At sixteen, Josiah had torn down and burned by fire the Baal and Asherah images. He also destroyed the Asherim, the high incense altars. He burned even the bones of the false prophets who had died. He was like the good sheriff in some of our old Westerns who comes to clean up the town (ridding it of all the outlaws). Yet danger was looming on the horizon. Babylon, the sleeping giant, an extremely wicked warrior nation, was poised to become the next world power. God would use them to punish His people. Because of the latter, Habakkuk would have a bone to pick with God. The crux of Habakkuk's argument was, How could You use a people more wicked than our people to punish us? God's answer, in so many words was that it was for Him to know. You will never really find out this side of eternity. Some words come to mind, spoken through Isaiah: "As the heavens are higher than the earth so are my ways higher than your ways and my thoughts than your thoughts" (Isa. 55:9,

NASB). Habakkuk was the only minor prophet never to mention God's people.[6] Instead, there is only a discourse by the prophet, followed by a response from Yahweh. Three such discourses appear, resulting in a dialogue between the two, not unheard of in Scripture. Jonah, for example, has a discourse with the Father in the fourth and final chapter of Jonah's prophecy. God, here, puts Habakkuk in his place with a rebuke, the response each time to Habakkuk's complaints—which occurs three times, a threefold exchange, therefore, between God and his prophet. Habakkuk makes two complaints and the Lord answers each with an explanation for why he does what he does. He also promises punishment for the Babylonians—a just reward for their unjust seizing of others' property. Will Habakkuk continue his plaintive tone? Where God, in the Jonah exchange, had to rebuke his prophet for a selfish unhappiness, Habakkuk ends in a beautiful and poetic expression of the prophet's thankfulness at God's justice. Ironically, while Jonah did not get the sinful satisfaction of seeing Israel's enemies punished (on the contrary, they were saved as their repentance proved them worthy in God's sight), Habakkuk did get to see his people's punishment. It was, therefore, perhaps easier for Habakkuk to end with a song in his heart than it was for Jonah who had a tough time of it throughout. Nevertheless, Jonah brought more misery upon himself by not accepting God's judgment and decision to offer forgiveness and salvation to Israel's worst enemy. Habakkuk, instead, brought joy and God's blessing upon himself by accepting and embracing God's judgment against his (and Habakkuk's) people for the present and against Babylon for the future. The joyous response of the prophet to God's stated decision recalls to mind God the Father's joyous proclamation of satisfaction with His Son (Matt. 3:17). Habakkuk's acceptance of the Lord's will and his decision to abide by it prefigures Jesus's prayer request of the Father in the garden of Gethsemane. Here Jesus had ended with, "Your will be done" (Matt. 26:39). When all was said and done, even Jesus had to accept the will of his Father in Heaven.

I think, of all the prophets, the close loving and trusting relationship between God and "embrace" more resembles the relationship between Jesus and His disciples. The sincere indignation, or at least the questioning tone in the prophet's voice, is not unlike the disciples wanting to know "when will these things happen?" (Luke 21:7 and Mark 13:4—a question about when the temple would be destroyed, which led to the deeper inquiry about what the end of times would be like). Habakkuk, then, would have fit right in sitting at the feet of his Lord and Savior. Instead, he looked forward, like all Old Testament believers, to the coming of the Messiah, just as he now, after his dialogue with the Lord, looked ahead to God's punishment of Judah, which, in turn, would bring justice for the oppressed.

The Literary Format of Using Dialogue to Convey God's Message

Besides walking with Adam, then Adam and Eve in the cool of the day in the garden, God also dialogued with his human companions before the fall. He conversed with Cain under dubious circumstances. He put Noah to work, giving him a divine commission for a job he needed done— to save a remnant of believers. Later, he conversed with the Patriarchs—Abraham, Isaac, and Jacob. Still later, he developed, and then nourished, a personal relationship between himself and Moses. With Moses, the Lord inaugurates the conversation between God and those with a prophetic office, leading up to our study.

Conversation was a regular part of the ministry of Elijah, moreover.

The fourth and final chapter of Jonah, as well, contains a conversation between God and Jonah as the latter keeps misstepping, necessitating reprimand after reprimand from God. We have mentioned others already also: Samuel, Elijah, Hosea, Isaiah, Jeremiah, Ezekiel, and Daniel.

The promise of punishment for Babylon in Habakkuk 2, furthermore, resembles the "oracle" against Babylon in Isaiah 13: "Babylon, the jewel of kingdoms, the glory of the Babylonians' pride, will be overthrown by God," Isaiah says in Isaiah 13:19 (NASB). "You [Babylon] have plotted the ruin of many peoples, shaming your own house and forfeiting your life," says Habakkuk in Habakkuk 2:10 (NIV).

"I Will Watch to See What He Will Say"

This, from 2:1, is an intriguing passage revealing much about the character of the prophet. The passage captures the joy of someone in a personal relationship with a perfect friend, a companion devoted to all that is good like no other.

Since the little book of Habakkuk is completely a dialogue, moreover, it appears to be amenable to a dramatic production. Aside from a conversation between the two characters (the only two in the book), we get this curious monologue. Here we can imagine the prophet looking out at the audience, addressing them, telling them how he is curious to see God's reaction. A statement like that rather sets the stage, creating anticipation, putting in cameo God's appearance and response. Those paying close attention will be on the edge of their seat to hear what the Lord has to say, just as Habakkuk must have been. The first thing God has to say is a gem in its own right.

"Write Down the Revelation"

This is from 2:2: "Record the vision and inscribe it on tablets, That the one who reads it may run." The passage gives

JAMES MANTHEY

us a rare bird's eye view into the writing and public reading process that would have gone on with all the books of the Bible. Since "Holy men of God spoke as they were moved by the Holy Ghost" (2 Pet. 1:21, NKJV), we will naturally be at least a little bit curious about the actual process. In the case of Jeremiah, we heard that he had a servant called Baruch who did much, if not all, of the actual writing (as described in Jeremiah 36:4–32). Jeremiah 36:6 also says something about the public reading aspect of the process. Sounds like the prophet would have dictated the book of Jeremiah and that of Lamentations to his assistant, then.

You can go back further, in fact, and recall that Moses, at least in the beginning of his ministry and leadership over Israel in Egypt, used Aaron as his mouthpiece until he developed more self-confidence. Exodus 4:15 ff. describes an instance. Exodus 4:28 ff. also has Moses delivering God's word to Aaron so that the latter, in turn, could speak it to the people.

Someone has said that the entire book of Deuteronomy is a tribute to God. In evidence also are the advances made by God through Moses. By this time, he was speaking for himself and doing so with admirable eloquence.[6]

We know that Paul later used a similar method with some of his epistles (eg, see Romans mention of Tertius filling this role).

Curious Hebraisms

Selah and *Shigionoth* are the two terms in mind. Some have stated their ideas on how these terms functioned during the Old Testament's version of praise and worship.[7]

Four Different Ways to Say, "I'm Afraid"

Habakkuk 3:16:

1) I heard, and my heart pounded.
2) My lips quivered at the sound.
3) Decay crept into my bones.
4) My legs trembled

Similarities with Other Prophets

The five woes between 2:6 and 2:19 remind us of those in other prophets. Isaiah 3:11:[8]

"Woe to the wicked" is only the beginning of many such warnings: 5:8, 5:11, 5:18, 5:20, 5:21, 5:22, 6:5, 10:1, and 10:5 reveal a pattern of finger pointing that some have mentioned.

Striking Figures of Speech Describing the Chaldean/ Babylonian Enemies

"[They have] horses swifter than leopards and keener than wolves" (1:8) (hyperbole).
"They fly like an eagle" (1:8) (simile).
"They collect captives like sand" (1:9) (simile).
"They will sweep through like wind" (1:11) (simile).

Habakkuk's Need for Divine Redress

When the prophet objects to God's chosen method of punishing the wickedness of His people (having them defeated by the Babylonians), he has set himself up for some divine chastisement. Yet chapter two, verse one (NASB) shows he is aware he has it coming: "I will keep watch to see what he will speak to me, and how I may reply when I am reproved." You might say this is a foreshadowing of the proper final response of humble acceptance of his and the Southern Kingdom's fate.

Three-Point Comparison: Habakkuk, Revelation, and Application

Habakkuk	Revelation	Application
"Lord, how long shall I cry and You will not hear?" (1:2)	"How long,… Holy and True, until You judge and avenge our blood?" (Rev. 6:10, NIV); souls of those who died early in Trib.)	But the fruit of the Spirit is love, joy, peace, patience (Gal. 5:22, NASB).
"I am going to do something in your days that you would not believe." (1:5, NIV)	He who was seated on the throne said: "I am making all things new." (Rev. 21:5)	God puts new wine in new bottles. The old is removed (Mark 2:22).
"Woe to him who builds his realm by unjust gain" (2:9, NIV); also: 1:12 (who builds a city with bloodshed), 1:15 (who gets his neighbor drunk), 1:6, 1:19 also.	Woe, woe oh great city great city, O Babylon." (18:10, also 18:16, 18:19)	The days of evil people are numbered. God has them numbered. The prophet is God's scorekeeper.

Questions

Choose one correct answer.

1. What is the format used in Habakkuk? (fight between the prophet and the devil/dialogue between Habakkuk and God)_____.

2. What is the outcome of God's rebuke for Habakkuk? He (accepts humbly/argues that it's not fair) _____
_____
_____

3. Name another prophet who gave a different final response to a rebuke from the Lord: (Jonah/Isaiah)
_____

4. With whom was Habakkuk a contemporary? (Samuel/Jeremiah) _____

5. What good king would Habakkuk have served? (Hezekiah/Josiah) _____

6. What bad king? (Jehoiakim/Ahab) _____
_____ What is one meaning of his name? ("God saves"/"embrace")_____
_____

How Habakkuk Still Applies to Our Lives

Christians throughout the ages have asked why God allows evil to hold such sway in the world. Believers will continue to pose such questions until the end of time. Some believers have fallen away over this question.

Others, some former believers and others not, remain skeptics, agnostic, or even atheistic due to this stumbling block. Christians in the know have grown in their faith realizing that sin, dating back to the fall of man in the garden, has separated us from God. Sin and rebellion from God have taken us so far away from a holy and righteous God that only the suffering, death, and resurrection of God's own Son, Jesus Christ, could offer us any hope of salvation.

Hebrew scholars translate Habakkuk's name as both "he wrestles" and "he embraces." Have you noticed how most, if not all, prophets and others in the Bible seem remarkably to live up to, or even grow into the meanings of their names? Habakkuk struggled with two ideas: First, he couldn't understand why God was not punishing his and Habakkuk's people for their blatant sin and wickedness. That was the wrestling part. Secondly, when God answered the first question with something arguably even more troubling, the prophet once again struggled (further wrestling). When God, finally, had answered all he was going to answer, the prophet, being a faithful and humble servant, could do nothing less than praise God and allow for his wisdom and judgment in the matter. That is the embrace part.

Habakkuk, therefore, teaches us it is all right to struggle and question the Lord as long as it's done in a spirit of loving and inquisitive pondering. Jacob struggled with an angel till he got what he was looking for (receiving a dislocated hip for his trouble in the process, however—perhaps some tough love discipline to remind him of his dubious legacy of past deceptions). The proper spirit would be as a child questions a parent why bad things happen or why they sometimes have to make a certain decision and then hold to them. When the youth hears that the decision is final, the loving and obedient child, just as a loving and obedient child of God, can only accept the parent's decision and final words on the matter.

Other biblical examples of blind, loving devotion and trust with the Lord come to mind: Noah, despite what appeared to be insanity by the world, never questioned God's plans or judgment. Instead, he went ahead and built the ark as told. God rewarded him and his family with preservation of their lives and with the distinction of being the new progenitors of the human race to follow. (Hebrews 11:7 describes this reward in as eloquent a way as you will ever hear.) Some have said that his one hundred years of building the ark involved somewhat of a prophetic preaching to the world. No one listened, however, except his family.

Habakkuk, finally, had the right spirit. We should look upon his example with love and affection. Here is a man who, like Jacob, was bold enough to struggle, yet devoted and humble enough to embrace God's will for his life.

Habakkuk

Habakkuk, "Embrace," the mystery man,
Three chapters, a gem;
In righteousness torn
By wickedness and violence that seem ignored.

He repeats the question
We have heard before:
"How long, oh Lord
Will you our nation endure?"

Our sins are many,
Your righteousness pure.
I wonder; is there any
Justice on earth?

He walked at the time of Jeremiah
Preceding the fall of David's city.
While the latter outlined the
Big picture, the former, in pity,

Dialogued with the Avenger,
The one slow to anger:
"The time's coming soon when[9]
Justice will not be a stranger."

A force from the north,
The Chaldeans, I'll send.
They'll prove my worth.
An enemy again

I'll use to punish
And answer your plea:
"Fierce and impetuous"
Their god is "me."

"Their horses are swift
And keener than wolves.
They will swoop like an eagle."
No mercy involved.

God's interlocutor, "Embrace"
This fact cannot fathom:
"Your eyes are too pure to let this take place"
He pleads, in his gloom.[10]

"How can a people
More wicked than we
Be allowed to topple
Us, and gain victory?"

Act two of this three-act book
Finds the righteous one perched on high,
Sees God giving his prophet a look
Of strange justice that's drawing nigh.

"Those who gain wealth from the sweat of another
Are doomed to fall," so don't bother
Yourself with needless worry.
Their time will come, and come with a flurry.

Act three, unmistakably cured,
Shows a prophet assured,
Appreciative and pure,
Humbled and immured

In the walls of his Lord's great love.
Hardly an ode more beautiful
Than Habakkuk's response—
Calm before storm:

How many ways can you say, "I'm scared?"
"Decay in my bones, quivering lips,
Deep down I trembled"
(To his fingertips).

Yet, with all said and done
He will "exult in the Lord"
Always again
He will accept God's word.

Notes

1. NIV Study Bible, 1379
2. Unger, 434
3. NIV Study Bible, 1379
4. Ibid.
5. *The New Unger's Bible Dictionary*, 717
6. NASB Study Bible, 1314
7. In *Prophets from the Old Testament*, page 137, Barber and Rasnake explain *Shigionoth* like this: "It refers to a highly emotional form of Hebrew poetry that was probably set to music and intended to be sung." They then make reference to the term as it appears at the beginning of chapter 3. These authors see it as a musical term, then, applying to a highly emotional type of lyric poetry, used to convey God's message in song. As for *selah*, the Amplified Bible inserts this phrase: "pause and calmly think about that" wherever *selah* occurs. Wikipedia adds "סֶלָה (also transliterated as *Selah*) is a word used seventy-four times in the Hebrew Bible— seventy-one times in the Psalms and three times in Habakkuk. The meaning of the word is not known, though various interpretations are given." The Amplified Bible's rendering will suffice for our purposes.
8. Barber et al, *Prophets of the Old Testament*, 87: Throughout his prophetic ministry he had pronounced

"woes…Perhaps…a righteous indignation…had subtly shifted in spiritual pride.")

9. God is speaking now.
10. Habakkuk 1:1

[note to layout: insert photo; centralize]

Of royal ancestry, and familiar with court circles, his three chapters are a warning to Judah that the Lord's Day of reckoning is imminent. Will we heed God's encouragement to prepare for His second coming?

Zephaniah

הגדול יום־יהוה קרוב

Near is the great day of the Lord.

—Zephaniah 1:14a (NASB)

HIS NAME MEANS "the Lord hides" or "the Lord protects." He may have been the fourth generation descendant of King Hezekiah and was, therefore, of royal ancestry.[1]

Zephaniah's ministry, like Habakkuk's, was during the reign of the reform-minded good King Josiah (640–609 BC). Some have argued, in addition, that he began his ministry during the same year as Jeremiah. Zephaniah, therefore, was serving the Lord around the time of Jeremiah, Ezekiel, Daniel, and Habakkuk. What a flurry of prophetic gifts and servanthood reserved for the time when Judah and Benjamin, God's remaining favored tribes, were on the cusp of God's punishment and captivity! It is as though, in His mercy, He offers them every possible chance for repentance. On the flip side, may they never say, after the fact (such as when they suffered their seventy-year captivity in Babylon, looking back in hindsight), that God did not warn them.

Like the children of Israel of old, their stubborn and stiff-necked forebears, they could only learn through the hard taskmaster of experience.

Before the Savior could be born from the promised remnant tribe, finally, they would have to be refined in the fires of tribulation and adversity.

The warnings in chapter three against Jerusalem, "the tyrannical city" (3:1) and the notation that "she heeded no voice" (1:2) nor did she "draw near to her God," point ahead to Jesus's same sentiments some six hundred plus years later: "Oh, Jerusalem, Jerusalem, you who kill the prophets" (Matt. 23:37 and Luke 13:34). Whoever said history does not repeat itself did not have this resemblance in mind. Both Zephaniah's and Christ's warnings for Jerusalem only, on a larger scale, finally, can be seen as pointed toward all mankind, on a divine appointment with his destiny for them at the end of times.

At the latter time, thankfully, all God's people will have realized the error of their ways, will have repented, and (if you are a pre-tribulation millennialist) a merciful God will have raptured you from the destruction to come. Zephaniah, as all the prophets, makes mention of the latter when he assures (at Zephaniah 3:12, NASB), "But I will leave among you a humble and lowly people, and they will take refuge in the name of the Lord." Praise God always for his mercy.

Three-Point Comparison: Zephaniah, Revelation, and Application

Zephaniah	Revelation	Application
"The remnant of Israel will do no wrong and tell no lies." (3:13a, NASB)	"No lie was found in their mouth. They [the Jewish believers, the 144, 000] are blameless." (Rev.14:5, NASB)	Whether Jew or Gentile, through the blood of the Lamb, we are all washed clean.
"The desert owl and the screech owl will roost on her [Nineveh's] columns." (2:9b, NASB)	"She [Babylon] has become a home for demons and a haunt for every evil spirit." (Rev. 18:2)	Would you rather live in a happy land of plenty or in a deserted land, a place of death? Seeing the curses for evil can work to instill in a believer a spiritually healthy appreciation for faith's rewards.

Zephaniah	Revelation	Application
"The whole world will be consumed by the fire of my jealous anger." (3:8c, NIV)	(to the seven angels) "Go, pour out the seven bowls of God's wrath on the earth." (16:1b, NIV)	The next time the world entices you to join in on their "fun" (sins against God), remember the wrath God is storing up for those who hate his righteousness.

Review Questions

Choose one.

1. What is the meaning of Zephaniah's name? ("the Lord reigns" or "the Lord rules"/ "the Lord hides" or "the Lord protects") _____ or _____ _____

2. Who may have been the prophet's great-great-grand-father? (Josiah/Hezekiah) _____

3. During what good king's reign did Zephaniah serve? (Josiah/David) _____

4. What is the time, therefore, for this prophet? (750–700 BC/640–609 BC) _____

5. Can you name at least three of the four prophets who may have been contemporaries of Zephaniah?

(Jeremiah, Jonah, Samuel, Ezekiel, Elijah, Daniel)
_____, _____, and

_____.

Why Zephaniah Still Matters

Whether things are going good or bad in our lives, we should be in daily prayer with our Lord and Savior. Being in a personal relationship with Jesus will also involve daily study of God's Word. When God joins us to him through prayer and his word, and our lives show the fruits of faith and a love for what is right, we will not lose sight of what things look like from God's perspective. Even when things looked better for Judah under good King Josiah, many of those who were supposed to have been God's people were not following the good lead of their king. We must remain faithful to the Lord whether or not our leaders are doing what is right according to the Word. God is looking for his people to be salt and light in a dark and fallen world (Matt. 5:13–14). A city set on a hill must not live in darkness, Jesus taught further, in the Sermon on the Mount (Matt. 5:14). "What fellowship has light with darkness?" the Apostle Paul adds (2 Cor. 6:17b, NASB). Whether you claim to be a Christian nation or whether you no longer care, God does not change. He still rewards the righteous, chastens his people who stray, and stores up wrath for the wicked. All enemies of Christ, God's Word and Jesus's righteousness will have their day of reckoning with a just and Holy God. When that day arrives, the ungodly will not "stand in the judgment, nor sinners in the assembly of the righteous" (Ps. 1:5, NASB).

Zephaniah

Nahum, Habakkuk, Zephaniah—
Three successive minor prophets
Each with three chapters; the
"Lord Hides"—

Zephaniah's name.
Of royal ancestry—
Hezekiah's great-grandson possibly
Serving under Josiah was he:

Though Josiah's reforms were well intended,
Like the righteousness of the people, they did not last.
Amidst threats from a Scythian invasion
His announcements left all aghast.

Zephaniah, son of Cushi,
From the latter 600s BC.
Paints a picture you soon will see,
Is a warning also for you and me:

When you send a mixed message to God—
A two-faced worship, a farce,
Upon your head he'll trod.
"Beware the day of the Lord."

Judah too is under the ax
Of revenge from a jealous God.
The Baals and stars have taxed
His patience; their wickedness old.

When we claim to be God's people
Yet entertain idols and more,
He will topple us from our steeple
Of church worship, not genuine at its core.

The "Day of the Lord"
Is a day of darkness and gloom.
Zephaniah minces no words.
Terror has entered the room.

Yet, hope's at the end of the tunnel
For those who sense the truth.
Be humble. Repent to Adonai, to El.
Perhaps you will escape his wrath.

As seen in Amos 1:8
More than a century before,
Philistine cities, great,
Are set apart for more.

Desolation! Gaza and
Ashkelon, Ashdod, and Ekron—
Death to a man
Seems to be his plan.

A return is coming for Judah
To claim the enemy's land.
Moab and Ammon, the
Two, will be squashed by vengeful hands.

Egyptians also will fall—
Assyria too, like them all.
As the remnant answers the call
God casts his vindictive pall.

"I am; there is no one besides me"
Like with pharaoh from Moses's day
Their arrogance will change to a plea
For mercy, but not today.

For Jerusalem: Prophet and priest,
Prince and judge, from top
On down, they will fall to the ground.
Their treachery God will stop.

The proud pruned away,
Judah's humble hold sway.
Jehovah has seized the day.
Those refined through mercy will stay.

Notes

1. Unger, page 428 for the meaning of his name. On the relationship to Hezekiah: NASB Study Bible, 13.

[note to layout: insert photo]

Haggai, with Zerubbabel (governor of Judah) and Joshua, high priest—encouragement from God to get the temple built

Haggai

להבנות   יהוה עת־בית עת־בא לא רו אמ

הזה   העם לאמר צבאות יהוה   אמר

[Thus] says the Lord of hosts, "This people say,
'The time has not come, even the time for the
house of the Lord to be rebuilt.'"

—Haggai 1:2 (NASB)

HIS NAME MEANS something like "festive." With only two
chapters, his book is the second shortest and third to last
book in the Old Testament. New Testament epistles like
Jude or 2 John or 3 John are outside the norm in regard to
their curtness. It is refreshing to know the Old Testament,
although often thought of as having lengthy tomes for
books, also has books where God got his message across
with relatively few words.[1]

Because of its place at the end of the Old Testament, it is one of the last prophetic words, or words of any kind in fact, from God before the roughly four-hundred-year intertestamental period.

Haggai delivered his message in four installments or visions during a four-month period. He received and delivered his message from August to December of 520 BC. Ezra 5:1 mentions Haggai along with Zechariah as prophesying at this time. This was the second year of Darius I the Great (522–486 BC)—responsible for the Behistun Inscription. Work on the temple had been halted for some sixteen years. During this time, Zerubbabel was governor (under Persian overlordship; Ezra 1:8–11) and Joshua was the high priest (Ezra 2:2; 3:1–13).[2]

The prophetic word from Haggai comes at a time when God's remnant had returned to their homeland. The seventy-year captivity and punishment period in Babylon had ended. The people had built themselves homes, laying the foundation for God's temple. Then the work had stopped. One easy excuse was that the Samaritans and other local enemies had acted in a hostile fashion toward them.[3]

In what may or may not be significant, the opening of Haggai's book says that the Lord spoke "through" Haggai (literally "by the hand of": ביד). In other prophets like Isaiah, Hosea, and Habakkuk, it says the word of the Lord "came to" (lit. "was": היה) these men. In a sense, then

God is saying that Haggai was the means through which He decided to get the people moving—to finish His temple. Haggai 1:14 (NASB) says, "So the Lord stirred up the spirit of Zerubbabel... and ...Joshua and... the remnant of the people."

Interesting also is that God tells them to go into the mountains to bring down timber. Such a command shows the trust He has in them now. The high places used to be places of idol worship and other evil practices. Now it is not a worry. These former practices have not tempted this generation unlike their grandparents and great grandparents.

Chapter 1 verse 12, the report of the people's obedience, is one of the most joyous verses in all the prophets. Christians love a happy conclusion. When Habakkuk questioned the justice of God's punishment upon Judah, we cringed. We wondered if Habakkuk would end up as another Jonah, a grudging messenger angry at his Lord and God. When, instead, Habakkuk ends his short book with an ode of praise to the Lord that few can rival for beauty and the joy of a faithful servant, our fear turns to joy, mirroring that of Habakkuk.

The history involved with a majority of the prophets had been the seemingly sad one of faithful men of God fulfilling their calling to reach out to the people, but the people either not listening or outright rejecting them. In the case of Jeremiah, the kings chained and tortured him. The

Babylonian conquerors found him in this pitiable condition
when the forces of Nebuchadnezzar finally broke through
the walls of Jerusalem. In the case of Isaiah, tradition has
it that wicked King Manasseh sawed him in half. Then we
come to Haggai—same place, but a much different time, a
much different people, and no wicked king.[4]

Haggai 1:12 (NASB) gives us the happy news:

> Then Zerubbabel the son of Shealtiel, and Joshua
> the son of Jehozadak, the high priest, with all the
> remnant of the people, obeyed the voice of the Lord
> their God, and the words of Haggai the prophet, as
> the Lord their God had sent him. And the people
> showed reverence for the Lord.

Haggai begins with a statement that goes to the crux
of his people's spiritual problem: the people are living in
luxury while God's house remains unbuilt. God's chosen
people, that is, are suffering from a deplorable lack of concern for God's will in their lives. The procrastinators are
whining: "The time has not yet come" (1:2, NASB).

Truly, the descendants of the remnant, over five hundred
years later, would also show symptoms of a similar spiritual
malaise. The Sadducees and Pharisees of Jesus's day were
blessed with the Messiah in their midst. Yet in their blindness from the comfort, luxury, and status they enjoyed, they

exchanged fool's gold for the true treasure—faith in Jesus Christ as their Messiah. In this way, then, Haggai's contemporaries foreshadow (at least until they were awakened from their spiritual stupor by Haggai) the spiritual blindness of the Jewish leaders of Jesus's day. It was a sinful worldliness and lack of spirituality that led to the persecution, arrest, suffering, and death of our Savior. Yet God was in control, as he intended it for our good. The rare and wonderful outcome of Haggai and Zechariah's preaching—that the majority of people saw God in their words and responded by building God's house—was thankfully also repeated over five hundred years later, in the conversion of many to Christ during his ministry. Thousands more followed after his death and resurrection as the apostles took the good news of the Gospel of Jesus Christ to both the Jewish and Gentile world.

Even the most difficult to convince, Jesus's own brothers and sisters, were brought into the kingdom of believers when they saw he had arisen. Jesus's previously doubting half-brother, James, became leader of the Jerusalem church.

Haggai, the "festive" one, reminds us that we all have plenty to celebrate as we eagerly await our arrival before the king in heaven on the day he comes calling.

Progression of Thought in the Four Messages

1. The people say, "The time has not come, even the time for the house of the Lord to be rebuilt" (Haggai 1:2b, NASB). What does a parent respond when a child says it's not time for them to mow the lawn yet? What do you say when they argue that they will do it later? The parent responds, "Excuse me? You will do it now!" God's response exactly: "Build my house for me," he says.

2. How does this temple compare to Solomon's temple of old? As the people begin to build, some of the older ones remember the grandeur of the old temple. The enemy had completely destroyed that temple, Solomon's temple, during the Babylonian siege. It's easy to imagine that they began to weep and be sad at the thought. "Don't worry," the leaders told them. This temple is only a shadow of the one we will all experience in heaven one day. Even Solomon's temple was only a type of the one to come.

3. As in the second message, this one comes in the form of a question. Can God consecrate something contaminated? Can someone defiled do service in the temple? These are rhetorical questions. The obvious answers are "no" in both cases. You cannot fully receive God's blessing where the people are still holding on to some kind of sin. They have been defiled. They need to purify themselves and stay that way.

4. God will shake the nations, overthrowing them. Psalm 46:6 (NASB) touches on this theme: "The nations made an uproar. The kingdoms tottered. He raised His voice. The earth melted." Psalm 2:4 (NASB) lets us in on the sovereign Lord's state of mind just before executing His punishment: "He who sits in the Heavens laughs. The Lord scoffs at them. Then he will speak to them in his anger." Just in case there is any lingering doubt whether God will protect what they are building, God tells them not to worry. Our politicians are convinced that for our nation to progress financially and in every other way, we must feel secure that our military is capable of defending us. We have the weapons poised and ready to answer any threat. That produces a good feeling of security for us all. Nehemiah, shaken out of complacency by a report of distressing conditions in post-captivity Jerusalem, came charging out of his comfort zone as cupbearer to a king and led the people, standing shoulder to shoulder with them in the trenches of wall restoration in the City of David, one hand on the spear, the other on a shovel. Haggai, the "festive" one, will celebrate with the people when they have completed all the final tasks and when they have restored Jerusalem as the special dwelling place of the Lord Most High.

Three-Point Comparison: Haggai, Revelation, And Application

Haggai	Revelation	Application
"Be strong, oh Zerubbabel…Be strong, O Joshua." (2:4b, ESV)	(to Philadelphia) "I have put before you an open door, that no one can shut." (3:8b, NASB)	Live a righteous life, trust in the Lord, then experience the power of the Lord in your life.
"I will fill this house [the new Temple then under construction] with glory, says the Lord of Hosts." (2:7b, NASB)	"The city [the New Jerusalem] has no need of sun or moon to shine on it, for the glory of God has illumined it." (21:23b, NASB)	When we live as children of light we let the Spirit prepare us for an eternity of the same, basking in the light of the Lamb.
"And in this place I will give peace, declares the Lord of Hosts." (2:9b, NASB)	"He will wipe away every tear from their eyes… There will no longer be any death." (21:4a, NASB)	God takes peace to an unheard of level in the lives of those he loves, through the Lamb, his Son.
"I smote you…yet you did not come back to me, declares the Lord." (2:17, NASB)	[to the church at Ephesus]: "You have left your first love." (2:4b, NASB)	God has many ways to get our attention when we need it—everything from a bang on the head to a prophet's pep talk.

Haggai	Revelation	Application
"The horses and their riders [of our enemies] will go down...by the sword of another." (2:22b, NASB)	"And another, a red horse, went out... It was granted to take peace...and that men would slay one another." (6:4a, NASB)	God's people can take comfort in knowing that their nonparticipation in Evil will remove them from people destined to self-destruction.

Haggai Review Questions

Review: The book of Haggai—third last book of the Bible, second shortest, but very important for restoration of God's people in preparation for the arrival of the Messiah. For people like us (who follow), we can see it as a preparation for the return of Christ to judge and rule his people.

Circle the correct response.

1. Haggai ministered during the 600s BC/the 500s BC.
2. Someone who prophesied at the same time as Haggai was Daniel/Zechariah.
3. In 538 BC, King Cyrus of Babylon/Persia issued a decree that the Jews should/ should not return to Israel.
4. Zerubbabel/Pontius Pilate was governor and Moses/ Joshua was high priest at the time of Haggai. They

worked with him to get God's people to rebuild the temple.

5. At first the people said, "Okay, we will build the temple"/ "It's not yet time to rebuild the temple."

6. At the end of Haggai's short (five-month) ministry, God said, "I will not bless this people"/ "I will be their God."

7. Because of the people's response to Haggai's first message, God told the people (through Haggai): "I am not yet ready to be your God again"/"I am with you."

8. Use this book to find historical background contemporary with Haggai: Jonah/Ezra.

9. Three people instrumental in getting God's people back to the task of completing God's temple were (Choose one set of three over the other) Haggai (prophet), Zerubbabel (governor), Joshua (high priest)/ Micah (prophet), Daniel (governor), Samuel (high priest).

10. One way God got the attention of the people (of Haggai's day) was by killing all their firstborn sons/ withholding the rain and not blessing their crops.

Haggai

Three names stand out in this short book:
Joshua, Haggai, Zerubbabel—
High priest, prophet, governor.
Two chapters only: Let's take a look.

Since prophets are needed when something's wrong,
Rest assured it would not take long
To find out why God sent Haggai
To post-captivity Jerusalem.

"The time has not yet come,"
Say the people.
When asked, "How come
You haven't restored the temple?"

The Lord is angry, that jealous God!
Themselves? Taken care of
While their Maker, their Lord,
They'd left unattended above.

They have sown but reaped little.
Their drink? Not enough.
Cold, though clothed, a riddle.
Wallets with holes! This is tough.

"Get wood from the mountains
To rebuild My house;"
So, when looking again
For much, in the course

Of your faithfulness,
You will not receive little!
Until now, you have received less
Due to faith that has been brittle.

The leaders! They are great!
The nation repents!
It is yet not too late
To make recompense.

The people show reverence.
The Lord exclaims,
"I'm with you," all;
Glorify my name.

A Messianic message,
"I'll shake all nations."
Let this statement presage
Jesus's exaltation.

"Kingdoms overthrown",
Chariots and riders
Going down
Like Egypt's soldiers.

Warriors of old.
The Lord may reward
With blessings untold
Those who keep his word.

Notes

1. NASB, 1326
2. Ibid., 1328
3. Ibid., 1326
4. It is interesting that the return and rebuilding of walls and temple took the people back to a time when they had no king. This was more like the theocracy God intends for his people.

[note to layout: insert photo; centralize]

A prophet and priest, given visions on the end of times.

Zechariah

רני   ושכנתי הנני־בא כי בת־ציון ושמחי   נאם־יהוה בתוכך

"Sing for joy and be glad, O daughter of Zion;
for behold I am coming; and I will dwell in your
midst," declares the Lord.

—Zechariah 2:10 (NASB)

IN ZECHARIAH, WE have another prophet who doubled as
a priest, not unlike Samuel, Jeremiah, and Ezekiel (and
some say, Joel). He was the son of Berechiah and grandson of Iddo. He, with his prominent family, was with those
who returned from Babylon with Zerubbabel (whose name
means "child of Babylon")—the latter, leader of the tribe of
Judah, who became governor. We often speak of him in the
same breath as Haggai. Haggai received his last prophecy
just two months before the ministry of Zechariah began.[1]

We can date both prophets with exactness. Zechariah's ministry began in 520 BC. God gave him, like Haggai, a message designed to instill urgency in the people to rebuild the temple and walls of Jerusalem. Since 538 BC, when the first group had returned under Cyrus (Neh. 12:4), work had lagged. High taxes and threats from without had brought the rebuilding efforts to a standstill. The people needed intercessors to remind them of their duty to God.[2]

Several features of this book point to Christ, at least by implication; Haggai, Zechariah, and their generation are proof that God intended to keep his promises of sending a messiah. The return of God's people was a miracle in itself—Persian Cyrus suddenly issuing a decree that is, perhaps, no less amazing than the post-WWII decision that allowed Jewish people from all over the world to return to the Promised Land of old. The return of God's people during Zechariah's time set the stage for the eventual birth of the Savior. The return of Jews to Israel in 1948 sets the stage for Christ's second return.

Undoubtedly, it is not a coincidence that God should give a prophet involved in the reestablishment of a Hebrew homeland several visions including allusions (eg, 2:10, 3:8, 6:13, 8:3) to a coming Savior. The Messiah was to come from the lineage of Judah, the main tribe that had gone off into captivity, and then returned to start all over again. Micah, some two hundred years earlier, had said he would come from Bethlehem "Ephrata."

Famous Passages

"'Not by might nor by power, but by my Spirit,' says the Lord (4:6b, NASB): The angel speaking to the prophet with words intended for Zerubbabel, governor, to remind all of God's ultimate responsibility and control over the rebuilding taking place.)

Messianic Prophecies

"'Behold I am coming and I will dwell in your [daughter of Zion's] midst,' declares the Lord." (2:10, NASB)

"Behold I am going to bring in my servant the Branch" (3:8b, NASB). "It is he, [the Branch], who will build the temple of the Lord, and He will be clothed with majesty and will sit and rule on His throne." (6:13, NIV); Jesus's second coming) "Thus says the Lord, 'I will return to Zion and will dwell in the midst of Jerusalem.'" (8:3a)

Messages of Rebuke, Inducements to Righteousness

"When you fasted and mourned in the fifth and seventh months these seventy years, was it for me that you fasted?" (The Lord's loaded question to the people, 7:5b)

Three-Point Comparison: Zechariah, Revelation, and Application

Zechariah	Revelation	Application
Behold, there was a man with a measuring line in his hand [to measure Jerusalem]. (2:1b)	Revelation Then I was given a measuring rod…"Rise and measure." (11:1, ESV)	We measure when we prepare to build; let us build on the foundation of Jesus Christ.
"For I," declares the Lord, "will be a wall of fire around her, and I will be the glory in her midst." (2:5)	"And the city has no need of the sun or of the moon… for the glory of God has illumined it, and its lamp is the Lamb." (21:23)	Jesus and the word light our path on this earth, leading us to an eternal light at the end of our earthly tunnel. "Your word is a lamp to my feet and a light to my path" (Ps. 119:105).
"Also [I see] two olive trees by it [the lampstand], one on the right side of the bowl and the other on its left side" (4:3)	"These [the two witnesses between the sixth and seventh trumpet of the tribulation] are the two olive trees." (11:4A)	The Holy Spirit empowers all who follow God's will— reading, sharing, and living out God's word.

Review Questions

Choose the correct answer.

1. Who besides Zechariah doubled as a priest and prophet?
    Name two. (Samuel, Ezekiel, Daniel, Elijah, Jonah)
    _____ and _____

    _____

2. Name the father and grandfather of Zechariah.
    (Berechiah and Iddo/ Jesse and Hezekiah) _____

    _____

3. What was going on in Judah when God called Zechariah
    to serve the Lord? (the fall of the southern kingdom
    to Babylon/ the people had returned from Babylonian
    captivity and needed prodding to follow the Lord's will
    for their lives) _____

4. What other prophet do Bible students mention, together
    with Zechariah, in the same breath? (Zephaniah/
    Haggai) _____

5. What year did Zechariah's time of prophecy begin,
    and what was the main purpose of his message to the
    people? (520 BC and prodding the people to rebuild
    the temple/ 722 BC and warning the northern king-
    dom of God's sending the Assyrians as punishment)
    _____ and _____

    _____

How Zechariah Still Applies to Our Lives Today

When the Lord promises to bless Jerusalem, saying it will be a city that needs no walls, it takes us back to a better time in the lives of some of us. Some of us look back to the days of small-town innocence when a person could leave their keys in the car with the doors unlocked and not worry. We could leave our homes unlocked even, at times, and still feel safe. In heaven, we will not have to worry about thieves breaking in and stealing (Matt. 6:20).

The New Jerusalem will be a place that needs no walls since Jesus and God the Father, along with God the Holy Spirit, are there to make sure it will be safe for eternity. Knowing that the place of many mansions reserved for us in eternity will always be safe should be a source of comfort, inspiration, self-confidence, and joy for us as we go about our days in this presently imperfect world.

Several strong allusions to the Lord, sometimes here called the Branch, make this prophetic message particularly poignant. We New Testament Christians know that having Christ in our hearts and the Holy Spirit living within us can also be a source of strength.

Confidence for us comes in this world, knowing that God will not allow us to be tempted beyond what we can bear. "God is our refuge and strength," Psalm 46 further assures us. Although we will have trials and temptations in this life, the Lord Jesus wants us to know he is with us. Praise God for his unfailing love.

God showed Zechariah (in chapter 3) Joshua, the high priest. The angel of the Lord was on one side, and Satan was on the left (attempting to accuse the priest). The Lord, our Intercessor and Advocate, intervened on Joshua's and our behalf, rebuking the enemy. We too can rebuke the enemy when he comes to accuse or attack our faith. The blood and resurrection of Christ, the promises of God, the protection God provides through angels such as surrounded the enemies of Elisha in a bygone era can fill us with confidence and joy to fight the good fight of faith God has laid out for those who love him (2 Timothy 4:7). Let Zechariah encourage you to restore your "temple," knowing that God will also dwell in your midst as he promised Israel he would do (in Zechariah 2:11).

Zechariah

In medias res this book starts out—[3]
Red horse in the night.
Others stand with riders too. A shout
(From an angelic guide): "All is right."

A question from Berechiah's son:
(It is what the prophets do)
"How long will you show no compassion
For David's city, for Judah too?"

Among the evening myrtle trees—
Reassuring words and true:
"My anger opposes those at ease;
With you my wrath is through."

Zechariah was son of a priest
Like others, we have heard of before:
His visions from Christ not the least
Of the Messianic strain. There is more.

"Why do the nations rage,
And the peoples plot in vain?"
(Psalm two, verse one maintains;
Words to heed, coming from a sage).

"I was only a little angry,"
(When they tried his patience so)
"Kiss the son," (with him agree)
When his wrath is "little," though,

Psalm two, verse twelve continues
With the theme just mentioned,
Spoken in a similar venue
For the wise (Zechariah one) words well intentioned.

Further visions, more to hear:
Four horns, a ram, meaning power.
These horns once turned on thee
Now wait for the enemies' hour.

Next vision: An angel with measuring line,
"The Lord will be our wall;
Jerusalem, Judah are mine.
Past enemies, humbled, fall."

Goyim from other lands[4]
Will share your place on high
When joined with us they band
At the end of these evil times.

Satan, is now our "accuser"
(The meaning of his name)
Of priest Joshua. The Lord (to the abuser):
"I rebuke you." It is over (his game).

"From filthy rags to clean,"
(The priest cleans up well, you see.)
Such words to a priest can also mean
We, too, gain victory.

Next a Messianic theme,
"A Branch (our Lord and Savior),
And a stone with seven eyes gleams;
The vine and figs we'll savor."

Good times for us draw near.
Angel and prophet engage again:
"Seven lamps, two olive trees—
What does the message mean?"

Words for our Zerubbabel—
"Neither by might nor power
[A famous passage, word of the hour]:
But by my spirit" (he yells).

"The two olive trees—
What are they?"
"You can't surmise?
My anointed witnesses!"

Some say it is the priest
And faithful governor,
Those leading the feast
Of faithfulness to the Lord.

"Ten by twenty cubits,
A flying scroll" is next.
A curse for sinners this?
(Who seldom do their best

To live in righteousness).
An ephah going to and fro,[5]
A woman inside is next.
Two other women, prepared to go

To "Shinar," luggage in tow.[6]
Now we see four chariots—
The visions fast, not slow:
A group out on patrol.

Other visions, other themes:
Symbolic crowns and hearts like flint.
Zion's peace. For enemies? Bad dreams.
Blessings for Judah and Ephraim,

A curse for Lebanon,
False prophets ashamed,
The Lord avenging Jerusalem
The King has restored his name.

Notes

1. *Nelson's Compact Bible Dictionary*, 651
2. NASB, 1332
3. The phrase "in medias res" comes from the Latin, meaning "in the middle of the thing." Some authors begin their accounts (prose or epic poetry, for instance) with little or no introduction, throwing the reader into the ocean, expecting him or her to find their own way to the details needed to piece together the bigger picture. Scholars often describe Homer, the ancient Greek poet, as the classical example from ancient literature. We should add the classic PAGAN example!
4. *Goyim* is Hebrew for "Gentiles" or non-Jews—an author's insertion.
5. The ephah may be a reference to a "godless commercialism" that may have "originated in Babylon." Merrill Unger, *The New Unger's Bible Dictionary* (Chicago: Moody Press, 1988),1186.
6. "Shinar" probably referring to southern Mesopotamia: This, together with the mention of the ephah, probably, once again, refer to the godless commercialism emanating from the Mesopotamian region, later site of Babylon. *The New Unger's Bible Dictionary* (Additional and New Material Copyright, 1988), 1186, "Shinar" reference. Shinar is mentioned in the table of nations, Genesis 10:10.

[Note to layout: Insert photo; centralize]

Malachi—the Lord's last Old Testament messenger, called to alert the people to His dissatisfaction with their hearts, worship and actions.

Malachi

בֵּן   וְאִם־אָב אֲדוֹנָיו וְעֶבֶד אָב יְכַבֵּד אֵיךְ אֲנִי

מוֹרָאִי אָמַר אֵיךְ אֲנִי וְאִם־אֲדוֹנִים כְּבוֹדִי שְׁמִי בּוֹזֵי הַכֹּהֲנִים לָכֶם צְבָאוֹת יְהוָה

> "A son honors *his* father and a servant his master.
> Then if I am a father, where is my honor? And if I
> am a master, where is my respect?' says the Lord of
> hosts to you, O priests who despise my name."

—Malachi 1:6 (NASB)

MALACHI MEANS "MY messenger." The date of the book is after Haggai and Zechariah (after 520 BC, therefore). In the context of Old Testament history, the temple had been completed by this time, and the priesthood and worship format had been in place when Malachi was called by the Lord to give notice of God's dissatisfaction with the hearts and practices of His people. Since Nehemiah returned to the Persian court in 433 BC, a good date for the book appears to be between 433–425 BC.[1]

Nehemiah, a probable contemporary of Malachi and leader of the mission to rebuild Jerusalem's walls, had also reprimanded the people for not bringing the tithe to the Lord (Neh. 13:10–14). Besides this stinginess of heart (3:8–10), the people are notified that God has seen their steady moral decline, especially rampant divorce (2:14) and intermarriage with pagans (2:10–12).

The fact that the people were bringing offerings to the temple means they were still performing, perhaps, many of the usual Sabbath requirements. That would be a good thing, except for the fact that the offerings they were bringing were not the best but rather the least they could muster. God's people should have remembered the lesson from Genesis in the story of Cain and Abel. Abel brought the proper first fruits and had a heart that was passionate to please the Lord. Hebrews 11 says that the resulting blessing upon him has lasted until this day in that we are still talking about him in glowing terms even though he is dead.

Cain, on the other hand, brought only an ill-prepared and incomplete offering. Not only that, his heart was further proved to be in the wrong place in that the jealousy against his brother eventually resulted in murder, leading to a life-long curse upon him. Since people were living into their 900s at the time, that is a long time to be under a curse!

Jesus told parables to illustrate a proper heart of appreciation and submission to God. In the story of the talents, for example, the one who hid his one talent and did nothing with it lost what he had and came under God's curse (Matt. 25:14–30). In another passage, Jesus quotes a prophet when He says, "This people honors me with their lips but their heart is far away from me" (Matt. 15:8 [NASB], a quote of Isaiah 29:13). The post-captivity remnant have lapsed into backsliding and outright disobedience to God's commands and plans for their lives. Enter Malachi, on a mission to provide a wake-up call for the final Old Testament generations poised to produce the prophesied ancestry for the Savior.

Well-Known Passages in Malachi

"Was not Esau Jacob's brother?" declares the Lord, "Yet I have loved Jacob; but I have hated Esau." (Mal. 1:2b-3a, NASB)

"Behold, I am going to send you Elijah the prophet before the coming of the great and terrible day of the Lord." (Mal. 4:5, NASB)

"He will restore the hearts of the fathers to their children and the hearts of the children to their fathers." (Mal. 4:6a)

Three Point Comparison: Malachi, Revelation, And Application

Malachi	Revelation	Application
"Who can endure the day of the Lord's coming? Who can stand when He appears?" (3:2)	"The rest [of those who followed the beast and the false prophet] were killed with the sword, which came from the mouth of Him who sat on the horse." (19:21)	"Therefore the wicked will not stand in the judgment, nor sinners in the assembly of the righteous." (Ps. 1:5)
"If I am a father, where is my honor? If I am a master, where is my respect?" (1:6b)	"I have this against you. You have lost your first love [to Ephesus church]." (2:4–5a)	You can fool some of the people some of time. You can't fool God any of the time.

Review Questions

Choose one.

1. What is the meaning (appropriate for God's prophet) of Malachi's name? "My (servant/prophet) _____."

2. At what point in their history was Judah at this time? (Returned from Babylon and showing signs of moral laxity/in the midst of material and kingdom prosperity) _____

   _____

3. For what purpose was Malachi called? (To warn the people of God's coming judgment and punishment/to call the people back to righteousness and away from moral laxity.) _____

   _____

4. Who was closer to being a contemporary of Malachi who had also reprimanded the people? Ezekiel/ Nehemiah _____

5. What is a good date for this book (within ten years)? (525/425 BC) _____

The Relevance Today of Malachi

Churches that mask a flickering heart for following Jesus's ways and words will sometimes hide behind an appearance of passionate religious formalism. God's Word says, "You will know them by their fruits" and "show me a faith without works and I will show you a faith that is dead" (James 2:18, 26). True followers of Christ will not only talk the talk, they will walk the walk. The invisible Christian church would never, for example, preach prosperity gospel over true law and gospel: sin, eternal damnation without Christ, and eternal salvation with Christ.

Malachi

Malachi, "my messenger"
Last voice from the past,
430s BC called to minister,
Final message meant to last.

Is your name a proper name
For a person who really lived?
Or just a generic one,
An anonymous man with a gift?

We will stick with the former.
A friend of Nehemiah?
Writing after the latter's return
From his first trip to Judah?

Let us look at the history
Preceding our *navih*.[2]
The background helps us see
The need for prophecy:

Haggai and Zechariah had completed their mission
To get the temple rebuilt.
Artaxerxes urged Ezra (in a Persian commission)
Godly worship to re-instill.

The latter occurred in 458 BC.
Ezra seven tells us all about that.
Seven years later Nehemiah came to see
That sin was cleaned up, righteousness stat.

Twenty-five years later, Nehemiah returned
To serve the Persian king.
With the governor gone, much went wrong.
Enter Malachi: to bring

Rebukes from Above, corrections needed,
A glimpse of the future,
Tough love for commands unheeded,
For sins past, a cure.

The pattern of prophets,
For six hundred years
Shows all why they're still needed—
We need mercy to avert guilty tears.

"I have loved you," says God.
"How so?" they respond.
"Esau is cursed," For Jacob
Blessings will unfold.

"Fathers and masters receive respect
And honor from sons and servants.
Yet me you despise and neglect:
Your offerings defiled, sacrifices suspect."

"Blind, lame, and sick—the worst you can find.
Give them to the governor." Are you out of your mind?
Adonai Tsebayoth, the Lord God of Hosts,
Has no use for your tokens, your empty boasts!

Adonai Tsebayoth saves His worst for the priests,
Those most responsible for these divine indignities.
Curses and ban! Blessings? No way!
The refuse from offerings, instead, I will spread over their face.

"Knowledge was to be preserved."
A task of the priest.
Punishments they now deserve
For treating God as the least.

The same holds today
For pastors and teachers.
I have heard James three: one say,
"Our judgment will be stricter."

Corruption and stumbling,
Is their legacy instead.
Unless they start changing
Their progeny will be dead.

"Life and peace were my gift before."
When Levites were pure,
When they could not do more
Than in faithfulness serve.

Pagans for wives?
God's daughters, betrayed?
Divorce, now in style?
Have we heard what God has said?

He is tired of perversions,
Of words twisted badly.
"How tired?" (Mock aspersions
To misunderstanding from sinners, sadly).

"Evil is good
In the sight of the Lord."
Words not as they should
Be – pagans' words.

"I'm sending my 'messenger'
To prepare the way"
Chapter three, verse one
Malachi will say.

More, a description in chapter three, verse one—
Of Jesus' messenger, "unworthy to untie his sandals undone."
"Who can endure the day of his coming?
We look for the second. Time is running.

Our Lord then as "Purifier of silver"
Will cleanse and deliver
Men fit for serving
Through mercy, deserving.

God knows what we are doing.
He sees every sin:
Swearing, adultering.
Cheaters will not win.

James five and four, offers us more:
A New Testament echo
Of Malachi's curse for
The worker-oppressor.

For those who fear giving
Will hurt them too much—
Chapter three: ten's "blessings"
You will get. "Open windows" and such.

"All the nations will call you blessed—"
God's promise to Abraham.[3]
Cast aside arrogance.
Yet some did not listen. How could they ever be guests

At God's home in heaven?
Those, instead, who feared and loved the Lord
Disregarded the leaven.
A "book of remembrance," a proof in word

They wrote to etch "in stone"
Saying that the true believers,
Those Messiah lovers—
Would end up in heaven—with all said and done.

Final verse, concerning the Son:
Takes us back to psalm one,
And the Genesis protoevangelium:
As the "Baptist" prepares all for "the One."[4]

Notes

1. *Unger's Bible Handbook*, 447 passim.
2. Transliteration of Hebrew word for "prophet."
3. NASB Study Bible, footnote on Malachi 3:12, page 1353
4. Ibid.

Responses to Review Questions

Samuel

SAMUEL'S NAME MEANS "asked of the Lord" (because his mother, Hannah, asked of the Lord for his birth). Saul was the son of Kish. The two wicked sons of Eli were Hophni and Phinehas. Scripture refers to them as "Sons of Belial," meaning sons of the devil. Samuel's three offices were prophet, priest, and judge.

Elijah

Elijah's name means "the Lord is my God." He lived in the ninth century BC. We find his story in 1 and 2 Kings. There is a statue of him on Mt. Carmel. His finest hour may have been in the face-off with Jezebel's 850 prophets of Baal and Asherah.

Elisha

Elisha means "my God saves" (in contrast with *Elijah*—"the Lord is my God"). Elisha served for about fifty years in the northern kingdom, succeeding his mentor, Elijah. Kings Elisha served under included Jehoram, Jehu, Jehoahaz, and Joash roughly during the years 850–800 BC. We first hear of Elisha in 1 Kings 19:16 where the Lord mentioned, during the cave encounter, Elijah's anointing of Elisha.

Isaiah

Many have called Isaiah, son of Amoz, the greatest of the writing prophets (Elijah and Elisha were not writing prophets). His name means "the Lord saves." A contemporary of Amos, Hosea, and Micah, his call to minister came in Isaiah chapter 6, when King Uzziah, a relative of Isaiah, had just died.

Jeremiah

His name means either "the Lord exalts," "the Lord establishes," or possibly "the Lord throws" or "hurls." Since there are several passages in the prophet that use the verb "to hurl," we can assume a pun would have been intended related to the meaning of his name "He hurls." Jeremiah comes from the Babylonian period. He was born in Anatoth, north of Jerusalem, in the territory of Benjamin. Called to the ministry in about 627 BC, God spoke through him during the last five kings of Judah leading up to the Babylonian invasion and captivity. He prophesied during the southern kingdom's decline and fall, that is.

Lamentations

The Hebrew title is *Ekah* ("How!"), the first word of the work. Both the Greek Septuagint and the Latin Vulgate translations attributed it to Jeremiah, "the weeping prophet." This book is included here mostly because English Bibles have placed it among the prophets, after Jeremiah, claimed author. The Hebrew Bible, instead, included it in the third section—the Ketuvim (or "writings"). The short book consists of a series of five poems, each poem allotted its own chapter.

Ezekiel

Ezekiel, whose name means "God strengthens," came from a Zadokite priestly family. His father was Buzi (1:3). Ezekiel's wife died during the siege of Jerusalem in 588 BC (24:1, 15–18). The Lord referred to this godly woman as "the desire of your eyes" (24:16).

Daniel

Daniel ("God is my judge") was a teenager in 605 BC when he and three of his young friends began the next stage of their lives. He served first under the Babylonians then under the Persians. In chapter nine, Daniel prays a prayer of remorse and confession for national sin. The book of Jeremiah inspired Daniel's prayer, accentuated by a personal visit from Gabriel, God's heavenly messenger.

Hosea

Hosea ("deliverance"), son of Beeri, served about the middle of the eighth century BC. He may have prophesied for about thirty-eight years, as the final years of the northern kingdom ended. While Amos credited an unnamed enemy with being poised to end the northern kingdom, Hosea identifies the enemy as Assyria. In the tumultuous last years of the kingdom, this prophet (the only writing prophet from the north) would have experienced six kings in a twenty-five-year period: enemies, their successors and accomplices, murdered Zechariah, Shallum, Pekahiah, and Pekah while in office.

Joel

Joel's name means "Yahweh is God." Scholars are not in agreement with when Joel lived since he gives no clue in the book of prophecy bearing his name. The choices are post-exilic (the more modern view) and about 800 BC.[1] Because of his mention of priestly information, many have thought Joel a priest. In that case, we could associate him with the likes of other prophet/priests: Samuel, Jeremiah, Ezekiel, and Zechariah. Joel is most often associated with the plague of locusts described in his book as a coming judgment from the Lord—sounding literal.

Amos

Amos ("burden bearer") was a simple shepherd from Tekoa, a hilly area about ten miles south of Jerusalem. Where Isaiah's beginning coincided with the death of King Uzziah (king of Judah), Amos was the main prophet during the latter's period of rule (765–750 BC). These were heady and prosperous days. Yet instead of giving God the glory and holding to God's Word in humility, there was corruption and idolatry everywhere.

Obadiah

Obadiah is the shortest prophecy and book of the Old Testament. Many want to put him shortly after Jerusalem's fall in 586 BC. Internal evidence, however, makes the reign of Jehoram (c. 848–841 BC) a more likely date for "the servant of the Lord" (meaning of his name).[2] The book is an invective against Edom. Edom was descended from Esau, brother of Jacob.

Jonah

Jonah's name means "dove." He was the son of Amittai, from Gath Hepher, about three miles northeast of Nazareth. "A short distance to the north of this site is located the traditional tomb of Jonah in a village called Meshhed." Jonah shortly preceded Amos under Jeroboam II (782–753 BC).

Micah

Micah's name means "who is like the Lord?" The capital of Israel, the northern kingdom, was Samaria. The capital of Judah, the southern kingdom, was Jerusalem. Out of three kings—Jotham, Ahaz, and Hezekiah—Hezekiah was the best. Ahaz was worst of the three kings during Micah's ministry. Someone has said Judah was guilty of sanctimonious orthodoxy, showing outward signs of obedience to establish worship but their hearts were not in it. Jotham did well in every way but getting rid of idol worship. The Assyrians defeated the northern kingdom. The Babylonians defeated the southern kingdom (over one hundred years later) and carried them away. The North never did return. The South, on the other hand, did return.

Nahum

Nahum, "comforter," or "consoler," came from a city named Elkosh. We do not know the exact location of Elkosh. The address to Judah, however, in 1:5 makes it likely Nahum was from Judah. His prophecy concerns the future demise of the Assyrian empire and its capital, Nineveh. Descriptions of Assyrian power make it likely that Nahum's ministry was between 661 and 612 (the fall of Assyria) BC.

Habakkuk

The format used in Habakkuk ("embrace") was a conversation between Habakkuk and God. The outcome of God's rebuke for Habakkuk was that he repented and praised God at the end. Another prophet who gave a different response to a rebuke from the Lord was Jonah—who sulked and complained, feeling sorry for himself. Habakkuk was a con-

temporary of Jeremiah. Josiah was a good king under whom
Habakkuk may have served. Jehoiakim was a bad king.

Zephaniah

Zephaniah, "the Lord hides" or "the Lord protects," may
have been the great-great-grandson of King Hezekiah and
was, therefore, of royal ancestry. His ministry was during
the reign of the reform-minded good King Josiah (640–
609 BC). Some have argued that he began his ministry during the same year as Jeremiah. "The Lord hides," therefore,
was serving the Lord around the time of Jeremiah, Ezekiel,
Daniel, and Habakkuk.

Haggai

Haggai ("festive") ministered during the 500s BC. Someone
who prophesied at the same time as Haggai was Zechariah.
In 538 BC, King Cyrus of Persia issued a decree that the
Jews should return to Israel. Zerubbabel was governor,
and Joshua was high priest at the time of Haggai. They
worked with him to get God's people to rebuild the temple.
"It's not yet time to rebuild the temple" is what the people were saying. At the end of Haggai's short (five-month)
ministry, God said, "I will be their God." Because of the
people's response to Haggai's first message, God told the

people (through Haggai): "I am with you." Use the book of Ezra to find historical background contemporary with Haggai. Three people instrumental in getting God's people back to the task of completing God's temple were Haggai (prophet), Zerubbabel (governor), and Joshua (high priest). One way God tried to get the attention of the people (of Haggai's day) was by withholding the rain and not blessing their crops.

Zechariah

In Zechariah ("the Lord remembers"), we have another prophet who doubled as a priest, not unlike Samuel, Jeremiah, and Ezekiel (and some say, possibly, Joel). He was the son of Berechiah and grandson of Iddo. He, with his prominent family, was with those who returned from Babylon with Zerubbabel—the latter, leader of the tribe of Judah, who became governor. We often speak of him in the same breath as Haggai. His ministry began in 520 BC. God gave him, like Haggai, a message designed to instill urgency in the people to rebuild the temple and walls of Jerusalem.

Malachi

Malachi means "my messenger." The date of the book is after Haggai and Zechariah. In the context of Old

Testament history, the temple had been completed by this time, and the priesthood and worship format had been in place when the Lord called Malachi to give notice of God's dissatisfaction with the hearts and the practices of His people. Since Nehemiah returned to the Persian court in 433 BC, and since Malachi makes mention of the same sins condemned by Nehemiah, a good date for the book appears to be between 433–425 BC.[3] Nehemiah, probably contemporary with Malachi and leader of the mission to rebuild Jerusalem's wall, had also reprimanded the people, as did Malachi, for not bringing the tithe to the Lord.

Notes

1. Unger, 403
2. Ibid., 413
3. Ibid., 447

Old Testament Prophets
Matching Assignment

Place the correct name of the prophet in the blank next to the description. Prophet bank: Samuel, Elijah, Elisha, Jonah, Hosea, Isaiah, Amos

1. Prophesied during the reign of King Uzziah. _____
    _____

2. 793–753 BC were the years of his service, during the reign of Jeroboam II, a wicked king._____

3. This prophet, priest, and judge had to deal with Eli's wicked sons._____

4. Seemingly suffering from signs of (what today would be called) manic depression, this prophet had to be reassured by a loving God that there were "still 7000 who have not bowed the knee to Baal."_____

5. The name James Bartley (who some claimed, by God's grace, to have survived a bizarre mishap at sea) should provide a hint regarding this reluctant servant of the Lord. _____

6. 858–793 would be the years of service for this man of God who left the plow, the oxen, and his family behind to follow his mentor and the Lord._____

7. His book actually (with fourteen) has more chapters than the major prophet, Daniel (with twelve), yet he is considered the first of "The Twelve" (minor prophets).

   _____

8. Wicked Ahab and Jezebel chased him for much of his ministry._____

9. Jezreel, Lo Ruhamah, and Lo Ammi all had their names changed to Jezreel (positive meaning), Ruhamah, and Ammi as a sign of God's mercy toward Israel and the man's family._____

10. God raptured him into heaven by a fiery chariot.

    _____

Old Testament Prophets
Matching Assignment
Answer Key

1. Amos
2. Jonah
3. Samuel
4. Elijah
5. Jonah
6. Elisha
7. Hosea
8. Elijah
9. Hosea
10. Elijah

Bibliography

Arthur, Kay. *How to Study Your Bible: Precept upon Precept*, Eugene, Oregon: Harvest House Publishers, ©1994, by Precept Ministries.

Barber, Wayne, Eddie Rasnake, and Richard Shepherd. *Life Principles from the Prophets of the Old Testament*, TN: AMG Publishers, ©1999 by Wayne A. Barber, Eddie Rasnake, and Richard L. Shepherd.

Barger, Eric. Quoted from presentation, session 10, "The Most Dangerous Cult" Great Lakes Prophecy Conference, Calvary Chapel, Appleton, Wisconsin, September 7, 2013.

Ferwerda, Julie, Crosswalk contributing editor, "Do Prophets Still Exist Today?" www.Crosswalk.com, 20 June, 2008.

Gutenberg Project for the license and permission to copy Dore prints of prophet images: This eBook is for the use of anyone anywhere at no cost and with almost no restrictions whatsoever. You may copy it, give it away or reuse it under the terms of the Project Gutenberg License included with this eBook or online at www.gutenberg.net

Dr. Hocking, David. "Can Israel Survive Current Negotiations?" speaking at the Great Lakes Prophecy Conference, Calvary Chapel, Appleton, Wisconsin, September 7, 2013.

NIV *Study Bible*, Grand Rapids, Michigan: Zondervan Publishing House, © 1995, by Zondervan Publishing House.

Quintana, Chris. "Modern Israel" speaking at the Great Lakes Prophecy Conference, Calvary Chapel, Appleton, Wisconsin, September 7, 2013.

Smith, Brittany, "Modern Day Prophets Exist, But Different Than Old Testament Ones," www.ChristianPost.com, March 20, 2012.

Sproul, R. C. *Knowing Scripture*, Downers Grove, Illinois: InterVarsity Press, ©1977, by Intervarsity Christian Fellowship.

"Understanding the Prophecy of Daniel's Seventy Weeks." www.NowTheEndBegins.com. 2009.

Unger, Merrill. *The New Unger's Bible Dictionary*. Edited by R. K. Harrison, Howard F. Vos, and Cyril J. Barber. Renewed by Pearl C. Unger 1985. Revised and Updated, 1988, with additional new material added. © 1988 by The Moody Bible Institute of Chicago.

Zondervan NASB *Study Bible*, Zondervan Publishing House, ©[Delete:1995 and insert 1999. By the Zondervan Corporation. General Editor, Kenneth Barker; Associate Editors, Donald Burdick, John Stek, Walter Wessel, Ronald Youngblood.

Wikipedia, the online encyclopedia

Youngblood, Ronald F., F. F. Bruce, and R. K. Harrison, eds. *Nelson's Compact Bible Dictionary*, Nashville, Tennessee. ©2004, by Thomas Nelson, Inc.

Index